Contents

Editorial iii

Allen Ginsberg introduces soft drugs 001
to Scottish Poetry c.1973
Stuart A Paterson

How to be the Perfect Romantic Poet 002
Liz Lochhead

Way back in the Paleolithic 004
Liz Lochhead

Monsieur Sax 007
Liz Lochhead

The Future 008
Rob A Mackenzie

What Poetry Can Do 009
AP Pullan

Two Black Grouse 010
Jim Carruth

The Unification Church of 011
Dr Robert Moog
Andy Jackson

Darien II 012
Ron Butlin

Prophet Peden rattles the 014
Prison Bars of the 21st Century
Ron Butlin

The Guinea Pig's Search for God 017
Rob A Mackenzie

States of Emergency 019
Lynnda Wardle

Beyond the Heliopause 026
Doug Johnstone

Renaissance 029
Joe McInnes

Dear Madam 035
Lindsay Macgregor

Frank 036
Claire Askew

Directions for burial 038
Claire Askew

Posthuman Jungian Analysis 040
Lindsay Macgregor

Balance O Pooer 041
Donald Adamson

Black Bull 042
Leonie M Dunlop

The Ge[...] 043
Ox of S[...]
Leonie M[...]

Thoch[...]
George[...]

Blow
Jim Carruth

Schoolmates 046
Jim Carruth

Lost Orchard 047
Jim Carruth

What Remains from 049
the collection The Way Out
Vicki Jarrett

The Chilean Way 055
Rodge Glass

The Whole Big Thing 065
Sue Reid Sexton

Dweezils Ripped My Flesh 069
Tim Turnbull

Sonnet for my Favourite Supermarket 074
Calum Rodger

what do the gaps in poems mean? 075
Andrew Blair

Is this poem going to consist 076
solely of the words...
Andrew Blair

Oranges Are Not the Only Fruit 077
(Thank Fuck)
Calum Rodger

Lyrical Commands 078
Nick-e Melville

Pigeonholes 083
Ian Newman

The Gutter Interview: 087
Liz Lochhead

Soondscapes 110
Christine De Luca

Wirkin tagidder 112
Christine De Luca

Light Show at the Botanics 114
Christine De Luca

An Appointment at 115
The National Library of Scotland
Kate Hendry

A Sleep 116
Russell Jones

Sylvia   117
Fran Baillie

Sestina of the House   118
Sally Evans

Boy   120
Stav Poleg

The Circus Always Makes me Cry   122
John Saunders

Holofernes   123
Stewart Sanderson

Asking   124
RA Davis

The Deil's Tell   125
Wendy Orr

Newhaven   127
Sinothile Baloyi

Auld An Yung   131
Hamish Scott

Enchanted Forest   133
Stephanie Brown

The shortest route on the map   138
is not the quickest
Pippa Goldschmidt

A Siege Inverted   144
Henry King

Not Climbing Mount Sion   145
Henry King

The Paddock-Stuil Stew   146
Jason Henderson

Rehearsals for the End of Time   148
Ron Butlin

Tripping   150
Alan Harkness

Life's a Goat   151
Joan Lennon

The Welsh Medievalist   152
Sally Evans

Yon hill ye descendit last year   153
wi the weans
Ross McGregor

September 2014   154
Peter Burnett

Extract from the novel *The Wolf Trial*   155
Neil Mackay

Reviews   166
Dear Gutter   181
Biographies   183

Editorial

Issue 13 turned out to be full of good fortune, as our inbox swelled with poem after excellent poem, many of which you can read in the subsequent pages. We were particularly delighted because we had already decided last year to ask three of Scotland's Makars (or laureates) to submit work for this issue, and is pleasing to see their poetry in the company of excellent work by other writers. A sign that poetry in Scotland is in excellent health.

As it turned out, the three – Liz Lochhead, the national Scots Makar, Jim Carruth, Poet Laureate of Glasgow, and Christine De Luca, the Edinburgh Makar – are joined by a fourth, Ron Butlin, who is Christine's predecessor in the Edinburgh role. There are some who question the necessity of 'public poets', but to use the example of Glasgow since the inception of the city laureate post in Glasgow in the 1990s, the public consciousness of poetry in the city has grown further and there is an enlarging, thriving grassroots poetry culture. Of course poetry would continue to exist without public money, it is a cheap art, but the existence of these positions and the dynamism of the individuals who occupy them are enablers for poetry, its creation, dissemination and reception.

We are also pleased to welcome back to Gutter, Rob A Mackenzie with a glimpse into his evolving, metaphysical 'Guinea Pig Sequence', Andy Jackson's mystic synthesiser, and Sally Evans with a pair of formal meditations on time and place.

Selecting poetry for *Gutter* is often something akin to being a DJ, curating the best tunes for a live set or a mixtape. During the reading phase, poems appear that relate, echo or merge thematically with other submissions. We don't set out with any theme in mind, but very often one presents itself and leads to the inclusion of poems that might not have worked in a different context. These themes (and the DJ analogy) become even more important when deciding the running order of work in the magazine. There needs to be a strong opener, themes are then built on and poems that somehow (stylistically, formally, topically, linguistically) relate segue seamlessly from the poem before. There then needs to be a sustained and interesting beat through the body of the set, some experimentation with genre and form, maybe some sampling. The pace and length have to be varied to prevent reader exhaustion, before building again to an interesting finale and a memorable encore.

Usually we keep these themes within the editorial team, they are simply aids to our job of selecting and sequencing, but on this occasion we thought we should share them with the readership. The first section of poetry, should probably be entitled 'Poets, Gods and Scotland'. Now those 'Gods' and 'Poets' could be one and the same, starting as it does with Stuart A Paterson's imaginings of Allen Ginsberg turning Macdiarmuid on to marijuana in

1973. We then come right up to date with Liz Lochhead's new poems exploring prehistoric art, iconography, daily drudgery ('bringing home the bacon) versus 'the howl', and the poetic persona. Then Rob A Mackenzie's vision of future poetry among the Twitterati gnostic Guinea Pig leads us into Ron Butlin's flagellation of Scottish history, its false economic prophets and its firebrand revolutionary ministers. The Reverend Mackenzie then returns with his gnostic guinea pig, before Andy Jackson offers us a synthesised epiphany courtesy of Dr Moog.

The second group of poems might be called 'The Human and the Geological', as it has at its core themes of the Earth from which we are drawn and to which we return, opening with 'Frank' by the very hotly tipped Claire Askew who Christine De Luca suggested for inclusion. The theme continues in Leonie Dunlop's poems of cattle and rocks –praised extremely highly by Liz Lochhead-, and Jim Carruth's complementary poem 'Blow'. The third section is quite simply 'Ludic' in its apparently aimless play with form, language and subject matter. But don't think that the play detracts from communicating the serious themes at these poems' hearts – whether it be the phatic slogans of late capitalism in Nick-e Melville's 'Lyrical Commands', or misogyny in Andrew Blair's poem-in-a-title. Our penultimate series is unified by domesticity, family and by exploration of memory, whether real as in pieces by Russell Jones, Stav Poleg and Sally Evans, or imagined as in 'Holofernes' by Stewart Sanderson, or Fran Baillie's sketch of Sylvia Plath's life in Dundonian Scots. The final poems return to landscape and nature, but with a strong injection of politics: Palestine-Israel in Henry King's recollections of his time there; Trident (Jason Henderson); the 'War or Terror' (Ron Butlin); and Scottish Independence (Peter Burnett).

While this Issue has a deliberate focus on poetry, we also have a boutique collection of excellent prose, both fiction and non-fiction, for you to enjoy. We were particularly moved by the searing honesty of Lynda Wardle's memoir of her time in 1980s South Africa 'States of Emergency'. Its haunting story of quietism and displacement activity is an refreshing counterpoint to the retrospective hero-narratives of certain progressive white South Africans from that time.

We are glad to see Joe McInnes's delicate Glaswegian prose in Gutter again, with his nuanced portrayal of teenage girl's artistic ambitions in 'Renaissance'. And perennial favourite Rodge Glass is back with an excerpt from his forthcoming, free-floating, intertextual novel 'The Chilean Way'. There is an impressive Gutter Debut from Sinothile Baloyi. And Tim Turnbull is back, riffing on artistic egomania with his Burroughsesque story 'Dweezils Ripped my Flesh'. Proving that Scots on the page should not be limited to poetry, Hamish Scott gives us a lovely historical two-hander between and grandfather and granddaughter in 'Auld an Yung'. The language is at times difficult, but persevere with your Chambers Concise Scots Dictionary and you will be rewarded with new insights into a way of seeing, a way of thinking about the world that is vanishing with every passing week.

For a younger writer, the difficulty of writing a short story or novel in Scots these days should not be underestimated. As we have said in previous editorials, the idiom of our grandparents' and parents' generation is disappearing fast. The fact that so little has been done at a national level to try and halt this cultural loss is a matter of serious concern. Recently however, moves are taking place to try and address this. So many of us have been conditioned by years of education to regard as slang something that Derrick McClure* described as a 'priceless national treasure' that we may be too late, but we were heartened to be invited in June 2015 to the launch of Creative Scotland's Scots Language Policy. Some impassioned discussion of which you can find in our author interview with Liz Lochhead this month.

It was an interesting event, with the literary entertainment provided by the other fantastic national treasure who is James Robertson. His readings nicely illustrated both how a knowledge Scots is still central to the way many people think, even without being aware of it, while at the same time addressing the confused cultural response that we often have to hearing 'that way of speaking' in a formal context like a government agency policy launch in the National Library of Scotland.

Robertson is a natural Scotophone (we can heartily recommend his translation of 'The Gruffalo' to initiates wishing a primer in the language…) and his readings and the warm response from the fellow Scots-speakers in the room (one of our editors, having had his 'ayes' and 'wees' knocked out of him at school was almost moved to tears at an official validation he never thought he would see) was in sharp contrast to certain of the assembled suited, Anglophone, metropolitan civil service and academic types who have only indirect access to that narrative. Our other concern is that while there was a lot of good feeling in the room, when one drills down into the Policy, the substance of it seemed a little vague with the major concrete proposal being the creation of a 'Scots Scriever' (Writer) in conjunction with the National Library of Scotland. We hope that the Scottish Goverment's Scots Language Strategy, to be published later this year, will make more resources widely available to promote Scots use and advocacy where it matters: in schools and workplaces.

While Creative Scotland has admirably stated that it will make communication in Scots possible in its day-to-day business, even allowing grant applications to be submitted in Scots, we remain concerned that this could end up simply as window-dressing, or worse, some sort of quota system leads to substandard projects being funded because they are in Scots. Care must be taken to oversee quality at all stages, a difficult task given the fragmented nature of the Scots community in the arts.

Part of the problem with Scots is that those of us that speak it are so effortlessly bilingual that we slip from one to the other without realising it and thus have trouble recognising that we speak two tongues. Linguists term this process 'code-switching', and anyone who has attended a state school in Scotland at any time in the past 150 years has learned to do it the moment they move from the playground to the classroom. But that does not mean that it is simply an accent, a vocal mask to be put on as camouflage in certain social situations and taken off whenever an authority figure is present. It can be *just the way* we speak. Of course English (or Scottish Standard English to give it its full title) is entrenched as the national language of business and education, but Scots needs to be given its due recognition as a cultural asset and valid mode of communication, not an object of snobbish mockery and cultural cringe unless it is being encountered on the stage or the poet's page.

A final concern for Scots is the lack of an orthography or standard phonetics. This is because Scots consists of about eight distinct dialects, which had never coalesced into an official state language prior to the current political union with England, whereas a gradual process of codification and norming occurred in English from the mid-18th century onwards. This has frequently led to internecine warfare between different Scots tribes over the correct way to spell the word for 'to' ('tae', 'ti', 'ty' being three examples) and others. There is also the perennial question of Lallans, the synthetic Scots created by Hugh MacDiarmid in a modernist grand project of historical dictionary mining. The language in Creative Scotland's Policy Document (set from English into Scots by the inestimable Liz Niven) has already caused controversy with some who identify as Scots writers by being too 'antique' and obscure, not the current idiom.

Yes, all language is mutable and change is inevitable, but these sideshows distract from the main threat: the loss of idiomatic speech, from which flows all poetry, narrative and drama in any language. We are reaching a stage now where a standard orthography might actually assist younger people in learning and remembering these idioms by writing them down. Other languages have done this in the past 100 years, why not Scots? Liz Lochhead, in her comprehensive interview with *Gutter* on page 86 says that the only way to preserve the resource that is Scots is to "use it... just write, write!". A tall order for those of us who are already losing our tongues, but standard resources like archives and some sort of orthography project might just help us to hold on before all we are left with instead of an idiom is an assortment of clichéd Stanley-Baxter-esque words and phrases like 'Gie it Laldy', 'Jings', 'Dreich' and 'Taps Aff!'

*McClure, J Derrick: *Why Scots Matters (3rd Edition); Saltire Society, Edinburgh, 2009.*

Allen Ginsberg introduces soft drugs to Scottish Poetry c.1973

Stuart A Paterson

Of legends, surely this is premium stuff.
Al Ginsberg, hipster, beardy lord of beats
jets into Scotland, bringing love & puff,
hep-scattergunning Scotia's staid retreats
of literature, gets Norman out his box,
shocks Sorley with his free verse blowbacks, leaves
Sid Smith translating Karma into Scots,
smokes rolled up poetry with Valda Grieve.

Chris hasn't smiled since he had lowping hives
(we're guessing but we think in '35).
The bearded hep god says to him, *what if,*
& offers him the misted king of spliffs.
Hours later, lost in some world-deep epistle,
a stoned man listens to a drunken thistle.

How to be the Perfect Romantic Poet

Liz Lochhead

Be born male.
Begin your career as a poet early.
Take advantage of your nursemaid's momentary distraction
by – not yet a twelvemonth –
crawling to the fire and snatching out a live coal, flamed
and glowing, learning
to brand Promethean sensation to your flesh and brain.
(This will also initiate you nicely into the twin satisfactions
of rousing the whole household with your shrieking
and getting a maid into trouble.)

Be orphaned ere you grow to double figures.
Ever after, idolise your father, disappoint your mother.
Have a sister (every Romantic poet worth his salt most certainly
has a sister.) She'll be the one to hearken when he sings
Come my sister, come I pray
With speed put on your woodland dress
And bring no book, for this one day
We'll give to idleness.)

Even if you are not Lord Byron
be mad and bad and dangerous to know.

Be faithful to your Muse and marry the wrong woman.
Your Muse will most fulsomely reward you.

When in London, lodge at the *Salutation and Cat,*
that hotbed of sedition. Thrill to that.

Leave your long black hair unpowdered,
wear your blue topcoat with a white swansdown waistcoat,
your mudded stockings most spectacularly bespattered – but
most vehemently refuse to change them just to please your wife.

Dream, but
ere you're older (if you want to get much older)
attempt to wean yourself of your predilection for laudanum, opium, brandy,
do drop the Kendall Black Drop for the more sedative stimulants
of egg-nogg and Oronoko tobacco.
Soar,
escape the real world of gruel, sulphur-ointment, haberdashery,
pig-iron, cotton manufactories and silk mills;
worship all winged creatures – Angels, Harpies,
the starling, sea-mew, ostrich, owl, canary, vulture,
the nightingale, sparrow, thrush, bustard, tom-tit, dove, duck, linnet, lark
and, ah,
the albatross...

Dread, above all, becalming, stasis.
Love the wild wave,
the humble birdlimed thornbush, let nature be your teacher
but be 'a library cormorant', dive deep.
When it thunders
run bareheaded, harebrained, out into the rain.
Miss all deadlines – write all night,
tempt and court the Nightmare and the Succubus
in pursuit of the green radiance,
in pursuit of the fugitive colours of the day.

Way back in the Paleolithic

Liz Lochhead

What do you know
Even then
In them Caves of Lascaux
Thirty seven thousand – thirty seven long thousand! – years ago
Way back in pre-history
This was already the essential mystery

Art, art, what is it for?

Ah
To create is to bring into being what never existed before.

It's that elemental
Artistic vibe
That binds us together as part of the tribe –
Every last sister, brother, father, mother,
Every born child,
Every man and every woman
Needed them animals on the cave walls
To define them as human.

Way, way back and long ago
In the caves of
Chauvet, Altamira and Lascaux
Those first – not-yet-artists – had to face
That blank wall that only Nature had so far had a go at
And somehow put it in its place.
So they bravely turned their hand to it,
Stencilling in its outline with the spatter and the spark
Of the spat and blown pigment
That drew so clearly where their hands both were and weren't
And they made their mark.

In the Cueva de las Manos
In the caves of Chauvet, Altamira and Lascaux
Already this fundamental inclination
That irresistible drive pro creation
Forcing those folk to fashion
Some form of ritual and religion
To carve and cut and gouge for hours and hours,
To laboriously smooth
And fashion the first art
In their fetishes of priapic phalluses,
In their amulets of big-bellied round-hipped split-vulva-ed Venuses
Art objects
Of clay, bone, antler, stone

For they knew man could not
Should not
Live by meat alone.

No they were
Not just hunters
Tasked with bringing home the bacon
But artists
With a mammoth undertaking!

Being human meant they
Must, they must, they must
Make images of aurochs, bulls and bison,
Fierce felines, fleet equines,
Bear and deer
From ochre and oxides and charcoal and mineral pigments,
Realer-than-real animals
From the life, from observation
And from imagination's figments.

(cont'd)

Because their truest impulse was
To *capture something*
Soon running wild on the walls were
Hordes of realer-than-real magical creatures
The flickering torches in the firelight
Transformed to the first motion pictures.

And did they dance?
Dance? They danced themselves to trance.
How do we know?
The bone flutes we found, the stone drumsticks tell us so.
In the firelight, in the cave,
All the other ordinary passing glories
Were the fugitive music and the stories

Their Art!
Art, what was it for?
To bring into being what never existed before.

Monsieur Sax

Liz Lochhead

Monsieur Sax, Monsieur Sax, the great Adolphe
You invented the howl of the urban wolf.
You made the saxotrumba, the saxotuba, the saxhorn
Then finally came up with that magical instrument that pure
Caught on!
Yeah, you tinkered with all that brassy trash and then –
Toute-suite –
You struck gold with the Daddy of them all who could sure
Toot sweet.
Though – as the cliche says –
You come from that place
Famous for nobody but Jacques Brel, the bloke that thought up Tintin and
Rene Magritte
It was you, it was you, it was you
Made that thing that makes that sound
That snarls from midnight Manhattan windows or curls
Like the steam from the grilles in the street,
The sound that howls its blue,
Blue loneliness then
Coos real low, cool and sweet.

All praise to Monsieur Sax, the blessed Adolphe
Who invented the authentic howl
Of the urban wolf.

The Future

Rob A Mackenzie

At times we wondered where emerging Scottish poets hid
between tweets, but we soon learned not to ask questions
affecting national security. They'd find ways to keep body
and soul together if we shut up: they'd caterwaul hymns
to hospital patients for half a crown an hour. Why don't
we update units of time like we update units of money?
An hour should be an anachronism by this time. If poets
were paid according to what they're worth, the literary
economy would flatline, leaving arts cash to manufacture
the four nuclear submarines politicians keep promising,
a writer-in-residence for each. Dontcha see the future
brightening like a golden sunset? The future is in capable
hands, between tweets. Headlines are a kind of poetry,
that's what we think. Shut up, everyone says, you don't
know anything, you just think things. Poetry collections,
they know, are a dying medium. Except, we think, for
the few who read them. No matter, check out the new
dot-to-dot sonnet spray-painted on a dying leopard.
The neon pink of a baboon's backside is a kind of poem,
doncha know? Check out the Higher English syllabus,
my ode to missile loaders. Oh, I'm so excited! Emerging
Scottish readers are the latest anachronism, between
updates. Why aren't people allocated celebrity status
just for reading a lot? Spoken Word is a kind of poetry,
that's what they know. Dontcha wish the future was hot
like poetry? We watch it brighten with a flash and bang.

What Poetry Can Do

AP Pullan

It's like that bit when the Angel Vera arrives
to take Jack and you're thinking but this is Corrie?
And you aren't religious or anything
but you like it all the same. Then you come out of it
in the ad for Cillit Bang and the noise of your kettle
but you're thinking about Vera
and you're thinking about Jack
and you're still wondering, as you stir your tea
how they'd be getting on
upstairs now, that is.

Two Black Grouse

Jim Carruth

During the killing times Peden the prophet
hid for days in the low hills above Sanqhuar.
Here we too look for some kind of sanctuary;
few words follow us, sodden steps for thoughts
walking an old coffin road, dropping from the col
to Cogshead, across Glenaber to the valley floor
where the green promise of moorland and pine
surrender themselves across the Wanlock Water:
colour sucked from a landscape abandoned by Dante
lifeless mines, pit heads, spoil heaps – hillside spent.

This short day has leaked its encouragement away.
We rest on the remnant walls of the lead smelter
its fire dead, gloom descending thick as coal dust
but for small flames flickering through the murk-
angry wattles belong to black grouse sentinels
who berate us from a pair of neighbouring bings.
We're caught between a coupled grief too close
for comfort, not letting us forget what lies before us.
There's no escaping the track to Wanlockhead,
nor what the stalking clouds on the ridge will bring

The Unification Church of Dr Robert Moog

Andy Jackson

'The illusion of choice is an indication of a lack of freedom.'
– Ken MacLeod

You've drunk denominations,
like a thirsty man who works his way
along the single malts behind the bar.
You've conformed and nonconformed,
lurched from Trappist isolation
to unhappy clapper, heard a priest
weep through a grille and wondered
who was whose confessor.

You've laid your hands on the radio,
waiting for the ministry that heals
but found neither God nor Devil
in the fug of backmasked voices.
But if there's room in your soul
for one more schism, step this way;
The Church of Christ, Synthesist,
welcomes you and all your noise,

saying *life is the great sine wave;*
peak follows trough follows peak.
You cannot shape its form, just
its frequency; amplify or damp it
if you will. There can be no peace
for you in the agonies of choice,
but here's our mantra of the week;
Attack. Sustain. Decay. Release.

Darien II

Ron Butlin

The Darien Scheme of 1698 was Scotland's attempt at creating an international trading company to rival those of the English and Dutch. Speculation gripped the country, many rich and poor invested all their savings. They lost everything. Of the original 1,200 men and women who colonised the Isthmus of Darien, only a few survived. Had they been able to google Panama before setting out, much misery might have been averted. Perhaps.

Real-time seems to pass too slowly?
Then defragment it.

If that doesn't work –

RUN a virus check.
QUARANTINE the Scottish gods who've hacked
into the system.

If that doesn't work –

- GOOGLE 'Financial Speculation:
  The Darien Scheme / Disaster, 1698'
- Print off each sorry A4 sheet
- Origami a fleet of paper boats
- Add 1,200 human lives for ballast
- Float the doomed armada 300+years into the past

UPLOAD the slurried, fever-ridden Panama swamps,
the gorged mosquitoes, the rats,
the snakes, the total lack of
anyone to trade with.
Most of all, the endless
tropical rain rain
rain and more rain.

UPLOAD the weight of Scottish gold
and silver coin (half the country's
hoarded wealth) stacked
and strongboxed on the nation's desktop
as on a green-baize gaming-table...

If that doesn't work –

SWITCH OFF at the mains and wait for 30 seconds.

REBOOT
Go to VIRUS VAULT
SELECT 'Scottish gods' and 'Unforgiveness'
Right-click both
DELETE

Meanwhile, Scottish history will have timed out.

REFRESH?

(Warning – Real-time does NOT repeat!)

Prophet Peden rattles the Prison Bars of the 21st Century

Ron Butlin

Rev. Alexander Peden [1626-86], also known as Prophet Peden, was a leading figure in the Covenanter movement. A hunted man, he preached in the open air and died while still on the run. The mask and wig he needed as disguise can be seen in the National Museum of Scotland.

From long before the moment of his birth he'd climbed
a stone-slabbed stairway rising
from the planet's core.

The sometimes layered sometimes molten rock, was all
the certainty he knew and needed.
God's Word mapped out the darkness
as a braille of clustered minerals, crystals,
precious stones.

Emerging at last into daylight.

Entering this roofless church, the earth.

*

From his crow's nest of a pulpit, Prophet Peden scans
the perpetual ebb and flow of mountain,
glaciated valley, moorland
(eternity has no shore to break upon,
not here).

We've assembled under open skies as on
God's outstretched palm,
our skin flayed to rawness
by the Scottish wind and rain –

Raising his arms to the heavens, Peden drives us forward.
Forward! Forward!

Until...

*

What unnamed continent is this? What century,
discovered upon whose unsteady palm (which might
at any moment clench into a fist,
to crush us all)?

As always, those who know are quick to tell us, quick
to help us navigate this ever-brand-new,
ever-better world.

We post our plans on Facebook,
tweet our feelings, our beliefs... Whatever.
We Favourite what matters most.
Retweet.

Our personal / professional /consumer profiles
are updated every hour.
We're LinkedIn, we're empowered!

Our enemies are quarantined safely
from our sight. Their severed nerves electrified.
The drowned are drowned over.

Guantanamo, Long Kesh, Auschwitz, Camp 16...

So many Calvaries to nail down conscience
on a daily basis.

(cont'd)

We live in God's name, any god at all
Whose blood flows thick enough
and black enough to serve
in the holy sacraments of Wall Street,
the Square Mile, Frankfurt, Beijing.

His litanies are the *Nikkei, Dax, Dow Jones...*

*

Prophet Peden rattles prison bars that
only he can see –
invisible breeze-block walls
and locked doors
guard against the threat of freefall.

A Covenant – here?

And so, back to that ice-hardened winter afternoon,
late January 1686, the parish of Sorn.
Back to that frozen riverbank, trampled-grass path,
that dripping cave –

Stone bed / bracken pillow / God's stairway
leading him down... down... down...

The Guinea Pig's Search for God

Rob A Mackenzie

The guinea pig has lost track of who it is or was
somewhere along the line, maybe before the line.
It dreams of South America but always of dark
rabbit holes which might as well be Rannoch Moor.
Minor troubles: lumps, thinning fur, the Internet's
fatal diagnosis; the guinea pig probes its bowl
for short-term solutions disguised as mark-down
parsley. Before the parsley... there is nothing
before the parsley until it stumbles across lemon-
scented woodshaving and social history is made.
Some experts believe the guinea pig probes
for God all its life but doesn't know it has a life.
It squeaks with angels. The angels lose track
around the time the guinea pig eats the *Daily Mail*
and crouches silently under a platform.

It would have been
difficult to explain
if anyone had asked,
exactly what we were
feeling at that time.
There seemed to be
no end to the creativity
of repression. Every
week more people were
locked up, disappeared,
found dead.

States of Emergency
Lynnda Wardle

States of Emergency

Lynnda Wardle

'*This is the year that people will talk about*
This is the year that people will be silent about
The old see the young die.
The foolish see the wise die.
The earth no longer produces, it devours.
The sky hurls down no rain, only iron.'
– Bertolt Brecht

I.

Sometime during 1986 I embarked on a period of kleptomania, which lasted for about four years. Mostly I stole books, although occasionally I would slip a lipstick into my pocket. I was a selective thief and lifted my treasures exclusively from De Jong's bookshop, a small independent bookseller situated over the road from the main campus of the University of the Witwatersrand in Johannesburg where I was completing my final year in comparative literature and African history.

De Jong's was dimly lit and crammed from floor to ceiling with books. The cluttered layout was perfect for a book thief. The air was dry with the smell of paper, pipe tobacco and strong coffee. In the dusty light I would go up close to the shelves, my nose almost touching the spines to see their titles. I was looking for Marx, Althusser, Engels, Bataille, Mapplethorp, just some of the books banned by the South African government, books containing the ideas that could provoke unrest and chaos and which the masses were forbidden from reading. Constantly under the long shadow of the Publications Control Board that dominated what we were and were not allowed to read, an afternoon in the murky stacks at De Jong's felt positively Parisian in its revolutionary transgressions.

Rumour had it that the owner, Marcus de Jong, a shy man with wire rimmed spectacles, was a police informer and certainly it was the only place we could buy books banned under the censorship legislation. But this rumour, like so many others of the time was part of the strange paranoia that continually crackled in the air and was never confirmed or denied. De Jong remained in business and those who bought from him paid cash leaving no paper trail for the security police to follow.

I sweated in my coat especially modified for thievery with extra pockets handsewn into the linings. I wanted to read these books of course, as many of them as I could, but in a country where certain books were forbidden and knowledge censored, I needed also to *own* them, to carry them away with me next to my body and to place them in an order of my own determining on my shelves. And buying them seemed tame compared to stealing them. Textbooks I bought. But these volumes I lifted, pocketed, and spirited away. Here in de Jong's they were mine for the taking; no questions asked.

2.

On the 12th June 1986, four days before the 10th anniversary of the Soweto riots, President P.W. Botha declared a State of Emergency across South Africa. The previous year, he had declared a partial state of emergency but his had not dampened the unrest nor the numbers of people being detained in police cells all over the country. Within the first six months of the 1985 State of Emergency, 575 people had been killed in political violence and more than half of those were killed by police. With the new State of Emergency in 1986, came new extraordinary powers to clamp down on news, information and dissent. News coverage of political events was restricted, curfews and banning of political gatherings became ordinary occurrences.

An estimated 26,000 people were detained during this period. The 1967 Terrorism Act allowed for indefinite detention without trial. Interrogation and torture were employed as a matter of course. By detaining key people in organisations like trade unions, political parties and community networks, the government hoped that the opposition would be fragmented and be less effective. In spite of the number of deaths that occurred in detention, morale in anti-apartheid organisations seemed to stay resolutely upbeat. 'There was no question they might kill me,' said Cedric Mayson, a detainee, in an interview many years later, 'that they might do anything to me, but we were going to win the struggle. It was a tremendous experience of faith which buoyed me up tremendously all the way through.'

3.

At about that time, say May of 1986, I was living in a large two-storey house on the corner of Honey Street and Lily Avenue in Berea. The suburb of Berea was once a well-to-do predominantly Jewish area, settled not long after the discovery of gold on the Witwatersrand in 1886.

By the 1980s Berea had slightly gone to seed in a genteel blowsy kind of way, a blurring of the edges, some houses falling into dilapidation slowly, their former owners having retreated further away into safer, whiter areas of suburbia. Berea was close to the edge where the city was beginning to reflect its future, the line between where blacks and whites could live according to the Group Areas Act of 1950 becoming increasingly blurred. It was one of the few white suburbs in the 1980s where black people were able to live, renting out rooms and flats from white friends who had signed leases on their behalf in what was becoming a 'grey area' in the discourse of the time. South African politicians liked to see all their issues in terms of colour.

As the middle class residents left Berea, a new mix of people moved into the spaces that opened up, an odd gathering of misfits who were constantly on the move – artists, musicians, young families, mixed race couples, drug dealers, students and political activists made it the kind of place that felt easy for me to live in. No-one stayed at an address for long; we were shifty and uncertain, insecure about rooting ourselves in a city where you wouldn't want to be pinned down, found out or classified.

It was as though the future had started to dream itself almost unnoticed, right in the heart of this tiny suburb under the noses of the apartheid *Baase.* Here it was easy to be visible and invisible at the same time. It was easy to be a student by day and then to slip into the flickering nightlife up Rockey Street, a ten minute walk away, lit up by acid and calmed down by joints that I had learned to roll with one hand from a travelling salesman who could simultaneously make a roley and change gear while steering his car with one knee.

This was the mood of Joburg in the mid 1980's, where everything seemed about to drop off the end of the world as we knew it. At the time I thought that the intensity of violence, political repression and paranoia could not escalate indefinitely but I did not know where the line marking the end of the world would finally be drawn. I did not know how to tip the balance other than to stay alert, be careful and keep moving. In one year I moved seven times.

4.

Halley's Comet streaked across the sky in February 1986. This was a time when information was thin on the ground, a time to read signs wherever we could find them. It was not lost on us that Halley's Comet, that red star shaking down disease, pestilence and war, had become visible at times of great turbulence in history: the Battle of Hastings, the Great Plague of London, Napoleon preparing for his fateful invasion of Russia. In Governor Van der Stel's Cape diary of 1682, he records a sighting of the comet linking it to 'heavy rains and an insect pest that has destroyed the crops. What will happen when the comet has sunk right down God Almighty alone can tell.'

According to my Calvinist middle class upbringing, the Bible was the clear about our state of sin and God's wrath. Even though I no longer attended Church or believed in these notions intellectually, during this time I became deeply superstitious. The Comet was a harbinger of something and I gave it the mystical attention it deserved.

Although the Comet had been visible for a few months in the early hours of the morning, what I remember is a warm April evening, climbing the hill to the latticed dome of the Yeoville water tower carrying a six pack of Black Label, a roll of blankets and a copy of the I Ching. The night was shrill with crickets as we stared into the sky trying to discern the trail of the Comet from millions of starry points. I threw coins on the blanket, squinting at the I Ching, deciphering the hexagram by torchlight. 'Listen here! I shouted to the company, trying to make myself heard above the noise of the party. 'It says that strength in the face of danger does not plunge ahead but bides its time.'

Still trying to see a sign in the sky, I later fell asleep.

The comet amounted only to a brief smudge across the sky that night; disappointing by all accounts. When I woke, shivering and hungover, I had missed the best of its fiery tail. I was like a disciple that couldn't stay awake in Gethsemane; as though some important moment had passed while I slept.

5.

By 1988, three years into the Emergency, I had finished my degree and was employed occasionally but was mostly out of work. I read newspapers and listened to the news on the SABC and it was as though I could hear the static silences where the truth had been censored. What the truth was, I could only piece together from other sources, but it was out there for sure, burning in the townships, hanging on a rope, slipping on the soap, falling from the 10th floor window of John Vorster Square.

It would have been difficult to explain if anyone had asked, exactly what we were feeling at that time. There seemed to be no end to the creativity of repression. Every week more people were locked up, disappeared, found dead. There were rumours of a sinister Third Force, an escalation of violence in the townships and rural areas that was ascribed by some to instigation by the police and army.

When I called my friend whose father was an editor for the *Rand Daily Mail*, the only opposition newspaper, I would wait for the click at the other end of the line before starting to speak, imagining the room full of plain clothes cops, ears plugged in and listening for betrayal in every breath.

6.

I broke up with my boyfriend and tried to be alone for a while. I befriended Jackie, a fey skinny girl, who introduced me to the barbiturates that would be my new solace: Nembutol, Seconal and Tuinol and to the doctor who would provide us with the prescriptions. I visited his office fortnightly, my weight now around 9 stone, my clothes hanging loose. He sat behind his desk, a bald dome with glasses. Jackie had told me that he was a morphine addict.

'How are you feeling today?' he would ask.

'Still anxious and I can't sleep,' I would say using the familiar script. It never occurred to me then that these might be real symptoms. And then, almost forgetting that Jackie had also instructed me to get Obex, the diet pills, for an occasional upper, I added, 'But I am still struggling to lose weight.'

One afternoon, with the sound of the air conditioner noisy and intrusive in the room, he said, 'I will have to examine you.' He waited discreetly for me to undress behind the curtain. I lay on the examination table, the paper towel crackling under my hips.

'Right,' he said, swirling the curtain back and bending over to examine me. His fingers were cool and I stiffened in surprise as he slipped them inside me. The air conditioner chugged above the drone of traffic in Jeppe Street and I lay very still. When he was done he straightened and wiped his hand on a piece of paper towel. I dressed and collected my prescription as usual from the elderly receptionist who I suspected may have been his mother.

7.

The question I asked myself was how could we live, what could I do, in in the face of this increasing political and personal chaos? Perhaps I never framed the problem in such a lucid way at the time, but my own shiftless days and lost nights were the avoidance of an answer, the shrinking back from a responsibility that I had no idea how to accept at the time.

8.

Most properties in suburban South Africa had what was known colloquially as the *boy's room,* or the *girl's room* where black domestic workers could live close to their employment so long as they had a Pass Book, an identity document allowing them to live and work in the white areas. In Honey Street, the servants' quarters was a low slung shabby outbuilding along the side fence. The tenants, a single family I think, or perhaps more than one, came and went without us ever having much interaction. Occasionally I would see a thin woman filling her plastic bucket with water from the garden tap, but mostly we had little contact and this just seemed to be the way it was.

If I had been in a different frame of life I might have got to know them better. I may even have employed the woman to work in the house. God knows there was plenty that could have been done. As it was, at that time I did not care about dirty floors or clean toilets. Occasionally I would leave a bag of fruit and vegetables at their door. Neither they nor I ever acknowledged the giving or receipt of these food parcels.

9.

My boyfriend, an aspiring poet and failed philosophy student, decided we should throw party. We turned the kitchen into a small shebeen and built campfires in the garden. I wore a skirt so tight that I could only take small shuffling steps, its tightness over my hips and thighs suddenly opening up in a flare at the knees. This detail is somehow important to mention, an old narcissism selecting the image to present as a view of myself as I was then.

Acid buzzed its way around my body as I wandered around the garden, its boundaries becoming increasingly unfamiliar the more stoned I became. Lit from behind by fire, was the man who was to be my next boyfriend singing Neil Young, his voice breaking with emotion. I touched the back of his neck as I walked past him in search of something that I couldn't remember.

Someone had set up a projector and Marilyn pouted and threw her head back in pleasure as *Some Like it Hot* flickered against the garden wall.

10.

If we went to bed that night I cannot remember. I cannot remember who left or who slept on the floor. What do I remember is that the next morning I was sitting on the back steps of the house wrapped in a thick blanket and drinking coffee with whisky, managing the comedown from the previous night. Leaning back in the early morning sun I listened to the ringing of the Sunday bells. I saw a small figure emerge from the servants' quarters, his hair tinged red with malnutrition, his nose crusted with snot. He had on a grey jersey, the sleeves too long for his skinny arms. As I watched he walked to the outside tap and filled a tin mug with water. I raised a hand, thinking I might say something to him but he did not glance in my direction or acknowledge my presence, and I dropped my hand again.

I saw with a sudden and absolute certainty that my neglect was the direct cause of his kwashiorkor belly, his streaming nose. I had to do something, I knew that things could not be allowed to slide any longer. I would speak to his mother and we would make a plan for his future. I told myself that I would ensure that the boy would be taken care of.

11.

When Monday came, life closed over me like water and I continued my existence – of being unemployed, of not taking responsibility, of getting high and getting by. I still saw the boy occasionally playing in the dust outside the servants' rooms, but still I did nothing about the dragging shame I felt at these moments.

Now when I look back I still do not have a clear explanation for my political apathy, my social neglect, my kleptomania or my addictions. Except to say that I know that these things were inexplicably linked.

12.

On the 8th of June 1990, the State of Emergency was finally lifted by President FW de Klerk. He had already announced plans to release Mandela and unban the African National Congress and other opposition political parties.

13.

Embedded in the word 'Emergency' is *emerge*, from the Latin root *emeger* which translates as to 'dip or to plunge', or to come into view from a place of darkness, concealment, confinement.

We had no idea at the time, but we were a mere four years away from emerging into democratic elections.

14.

Jackie died of an overdose. I delivered the pills to her late one Friday afternoon and didn't stop to get high with her. I wished I had, and I was grateful I hadn't.

After she died, it was as though a very bright light had been shone into the corners of my shabby, neglectful existence. I cannot say that I never took drugs after her death, that would have been too easy an epiphany, but I never touched barbiturates again. Soon after, I was employed by the local library and worked there for the next ten years, my life held fast by books once again. But in reality it was shame that was my new barometer to test my actions in the world, to see whether or not I was really alive.

Beyond the Heliopause

Doug Johnstone

'Acknowledge the moon
It was part of the earth once
Its loneliness can make you feel beautiful'
'Be Prepared', William Letford

She cried when she read about Voyager. Tears down her face as she pushed her bare feet into the sand and stared at her phone. It didn't help that she was sitting on a beach 11,688 miles from home. She knew the exact figure from an app, the number going up the whole time she was travelling. And now she'd found out she had a kindred spirit in Voyager-1. She read the first sentence of the news story again.

'The Voyager-1 spacecraft has become the first manmade object to leave the Solar System.'

The details killed her. It had been travelling through space for thirty-six years, twice as long as she'd been alive. It was almost twelve billion miles from home. Its radio signal took seventeen hours to get back to earth. Sensors on the probe had indicated a change in its environment, so scientists knew it had breached the edge of the solar system, where the power of the sun waned. It had broken through the heliopause. A beautiful word.

Voyager was now in deep space.

Her plan had been to go to the opposite side of the world from where he did it. There was a word for it, two diametrically opposite places on earth were called 'antipodes'. Another beautiful word. Imagine the extremes linked through the molten centre of the planet by a single, delicate thread.

It was impossible to get to her antipode. When she put in the coordinates for Portobello in Edinburgh, its opposite was in the middle of the Southern Ocean, halfway between New Zealand and the Antarctic. She zoomed out on the map and found the nearest settlement, Dunedin in southeast New Zealand. Re-centred the map, zoomed back in and her heart thumped. A few miles east of Dunedin was a tiny seaside village called Portobello. She didn't believe in signs but this was something to aim for, a purpose to carry her away.

So here she was crying on a different Portobello beach. He used to tell her that she thought too much, how could you think too much? But he was right. That's why she liked numbers, they helped fill her mind with facts, not thoughts. But the thoughts kept coming, and being on the other side of the world didn't change that.

She had his old albums on her phone, all that melancholic country rock, Wilco,

Smog, Sparklehorse, beautiful songs about sadness and death. When she wanted to finger the wound she put those albums on. It hurt, but it was a link to him all the same, an echo of their lives.

You never escaped. Look at Voyager, billions of miles from home and still in touch. She clicked on a link from the news story, went through to a NASA website called Where Are The Voyagers? It said Voyager-1's distance from earth was 18,863,477,410 km. And it was going up every moment, seventeen kilometres a second. Beneath that was another number, 126.09457702 AU, also increasing. AU was astronomical units, the average earth-sun distance, 93 million miles, so that little soul was one hundred and twenty-six times the distance of the sun away.

It was almost dark now on the beach, a half-moon in the corner of the sky trying to bounce the sun's power back to earth. She looked round. Low green hills in the distance, dark water in the bay, stumpy trees and bushes. It could've been Scotland.

What were you supposed to do when your dad killed himself a month after your mum died of cancer? Leaving a note saying he couldn't go on without her. Leaving his teenage daughter alone. What were you supposed to do with that? Take a pill, go to therapy?

She swiped through the camera roll on her phone. She'd scanned loads of old pictures, looking for signs, a glint in their wedding photos or holiday snaps, something in the eyes that knew all this would turn to dust in a few years. But of course there was nothing, just a happy, smiling couple waiting for life to happen to them.

She took the box out of her bag. He'd travelled round the planet in there. She hadn't known what to do with his ashes before, but now, on the beach, it came to her.

She put her phone and the box down and stood up. Pulled her jeans and T-shirt off, then bra and pants. She picked up the box and walked into the water. The cold grabbed her legs as she went deeper. She imagined icebergs not far away, lonely out in the ocean, searching for landfall.

She ducked under the water, began to swim, the box still in her fist. She surfaced, the coldness pummelling the breath from her. She felt alive for the first time in ages. She looked at the moon, weak light sprinkled on the ripples she made. She remembered a line from a poem about the moon she'd read somewhere, how its loneliness can make you feel beautiful. She wanted to feel beautiful.

She took a breath and dived down. She went deeper, unsure how far away the bottom was. Already the moonlight couldn't reach her, she was swimming blind in frozen blackness. Her lungs burned as she kicked down, currents around her, until finally she felt sand. She pushed the box into the sand then kicked up, the oxygen in her blood dissipating, dizziness coming over her. The urge to open her mouth and let the ocean fill her was overwhelming. She pushed upwards, her torso rigid, then broke the surface with a cough, gulped in air.

Her arms and head shook, cramp stretched along her calves and thighs. She saw the shore in the moonlight, her little pile of clothes, and headed towards it. She winced as more cramp spread through her body, but she kicked through it.

She felt sand under her feet, stumbled and waded out the bay, her body convulsing. The lack of control was liberating.

She slumped down shivering next to her clothes and looked out to sea.

'Bye, Dad.'

She picked up her phone and went to Where Are The Voyagers? Looked at the number, 18,863,504,289 km and rising. It had already travelled further since she last looked than she was from home.

She imagined being out there beyond the heliopause, exploring the vastness of space, sending her signal back home to anyone who would listen.

Renaissance
Extract from a novel

Joe McInnes

Mr Carvil wis showin us a book ae Leonardo Da Vinci drawins. Ther wis hunners ae sketches, but the teacher wanted us tae concentrate on the anatomy wans. Drawins ae skulls wi big black holes wher the eyes should ae been. Ye'd never believe how massive yer eye sockets are. Ther wis pictures ae skeletons an other wans ae hands an feet. Some wer diagrams ae hearts an intestines. Ther wis this wan page wi lots ae drawins ae a guy's shoulder an wance Mr Carvil showed us Leonardo's paintin ae Saint Jerome, ye could see how his sketches related tae his finished work. Ther wis wan drawin ae a wee toaty wean inside this capsule kind ae thing.

If ye can train yoursels tae be as concerned wi anatomy as Da Vinci ye won't go far wrong, says the art teacher.

Wher did Leonardo get his models from sir? somedae asks.

He sketched dissected cadavers, says Mr Carvil. Corpses that is, in order tae study human anatomy.

Are ye sayin he used deid body's sir? I asks.

Aye, he goes. That's exactly what I'm sayin.

Some people in the class acted as if they wer pure disgusted but it didnae bother me. Cause wance ye looked at Leonardo's drawins it helped ye understand yer own stuff. For talkin sake ye could see how fingers wer joined up intae aw different bits. Yer feet tae an yer legs an arms. How yer shoulder blades an rib cage wer attached tae yer spine. In fact yer whole body for that matter, wan bit joined up tae the next.

The teacher handed oot photocopies ae the drawins an told us tae choose wan an make a sketch. I decided tae copy the wee wean, an embryo, Mr Carvil called it an he tritae persuade me tae draw someten else.

But ye says we can pick any drawin we want sir, I goes.

I thought ye would ae choose someten wi more artistic value, he goes.

I knew he meant the arms an legs an skulls an stuff, cause that would ae came in handy for figure drawin. But I drew the wean anyway. I mean weans are figures tae. Its shape wis aw circles, a wee wan for the heid an a bigger wan for the body an a bigger wan again for the womb. Leonardo had shaded his drawin wi spherical lines, but on the part ae the heid that wis cuddled intae the knees it looked as he had left the paper blank.

I showed it tae Mr Carvil an he told me Leonardo had put down a ground coat before makin his drawin in silverpoint, cause that's what they used in those days.

The renaissance, the art teacher called it.

Wance we had finished our drawins he began talkin aboot art school. Ther wis aboot twelve ae us in the class, aw fifth years. Most ae ma classmates wer only ther cause they needed higher art tae get a place at college. Ther wis three ae us in the class supposed tae be applyin tae art school. Mr Carvil had awready spoke tae ma Da aboot it last term. He tritae persuade the higher art wans tae apply, but aw they cared aboot wis gettin a qualification for college.

Ae the three ae us tritae get intae art school I wis the only lassie. The two bhoys wer Ian Barr an Stuart Anderson. We'd awready got our higher art in fourth year. Ian wis mostly intae paintin, even though Mr Carvil preferred us tae stick tae drawin. He wis good wi colours though an done a lot ae abstract stuff. Stuart concentrated on his drawin but he wis good at figures. The three ae us got on well an showed each other our stuff. But the two ae them wer more close probably cause I wis a lassie.

The most important part ae yer application is yer portfolio, the teacher says.

Can we submit paintins? asks Ian.

Ye can submit work in any media, as long as it reveals yer creative process. Mr Carvil goes. Ye should also include yer sketchbooks, so ye can show wher ye got yer ideas from an how yer work developed.

I've got hunners ae sketchbooks, says Stuart.

Another thing I should mention, Mr Carvil looked at me as he wis talkin. Ye need tae include a commentary on yer portfolio.

That wis the bit I hated, havin tae write aboot yer stuff. Reflective writin it's called. It disnae make any sense. For wan thing I'm hopeless at writin. As if things wernae bad enough havin tae re-sit ma english higher.

A commentary, I goes.

The tutors want tae assess yer work in context, the teacher says. Aw ye have tae dae is write aboot why ye choose a specific subject. Or ye could attempt a more general commentary on what motivates ye tae draw in the first place.

Life wouldnae be worth livin wi oot drawin, I says.

That's the kind ae thing ther lookin for, he says. But mibbe expressed in more objective language.

I'd awready had a wan-tae-wan wi Mr Carvil on what tae submit. He told me I shouldnae have any trouble wi ma still lives an cityscapes. But In the meantime I should concentrate on figure an portrait drawin an he would arrange a life drawin class for me tae attend.

I'm no against ye drawin from photographs Mhari, he'd says. But it's no enough.

Mr Carvil didnae come right oot an say it but I knew what he meant. Ye cannae capture a person deep doon from a photo. An as far as I'm concerned that's what makes a drawin in the first place. Aye, it's important tae learn aw the technical stuff aboot what goes wher on somedae's face. But see if ye cannae show the core ae the person yer finished piece disnae have any depth.

The bell went an I packed ma stuff away. I wis glad it wis the last class ae the day cause I'd been given a lot tae think aboot. I mean I'd been sweatin it ever since I found oot I had tae re-sit ma english higher. But I wis takin a whitey at the thought ae havin tae write someten for ma portfolio. I'd never get a place at art school at this rate. But like I told ye, nobodae had even bothered askin me if I wanted tae go ther in the first place.

Ma Da wis sittin watchin *Countdown* wance I got home from school. He had a pen an pad in front ae him tritae work oot the numbers game. He wis pure caught up in it so I went intae ma bedroom. At first I sat on top ae ma bed wi ma sketchpad open but ma mind wisnae in it. I checked ma mobile tae see if I had any messages. Ever since Saturday nite I kept thinkin Danny wis gonnae text me. I hadnae heard from Janie either. She disnae have any the same classes as me on a Monday but she usually sends me a text. I wis fed up an pulled the quilt over me an before I knew it I fell asleep.

Mhari, I woke up wi ma Da chappin ma bedroom door. Yer dinners ready.

Ma Da always makes spaghetti an chips on a Monday. He likes tae stick tae a routine wi his cookin. We ate our dinner watchin the *Weakest Link*. Ma Da wis answerin aw the questions an shoutin, Ya idiot, at the wans gettin ther questions wrong.

It's no as easy as if yer on the telly Da, I says.

I felt sorry for the contestant's when they did the 'Walk ae Shame'. But if they slagged aff the wans left on I didnae feel as bad.

After ma dinner I decided tae have a bath while ma Da watched *Scotland Today*. I took ma mobile intae the bathroom wi me an put it on top ae the cistern. I always tritae make sure the waters pure roastin when I run a bath so I can just lie an soak. Wance the water cools doon I duck ma heid under tae wash ma hair.

So ther I wis wi ma heid under the water holdin ma nose when I heard ma Da shoutin someten ootside the bathroom door. I couldnae make oot what he wis sayin cause his voice wis aw distorted. I lifted ma heid oot ae the water.

I cannae hear ye Da, I shouts.

Thers a bhoy at the door for ye, he goes.

A bhoy, I goes. At this door?

Aye, ma Da says. Dae ye want me tae bring him in?

I jumped oot the bath like a maddie, splashin water aw over the place. I pulled a towel roon me an opened the toilet door just enough tae see ma Da standin ther. He had a wee grin on his face.

Who is it? I mouthed tae him considerin how near our front door is tae our bathroom.

Just some bhoy, Ma Da opened his palms an shrugged.

Da, I whispered. I'm feart.

Don't be daft Mhari, he whispered back. It's him came roon here lookin for you.

What'll I dae? I asks.

Just take yer time gettin ready, he says. I'll bring him intae the livin room an make a cup ae tea.

Ma Da pulled the bathroom door shut an I dried masel at a-hunner-mile-an-hour. It must be Danny, I thought, who else could it be? I'd better hurry up an get oot ther before he put me in it for Saturday nite. I skidaddled doon the hall an intae ma bedroom wi a towel wrapped roon me. I wis ready like a shot an wance I walked intae the livin room Danny wis sittin on the couch.

Ye'll have tae come roon more often Danny, ma Da says. I've never seen her gettin ready so fast.

How'd ye know wher I lived? I says, sittin on the arm ae ma Da's chair. Ye should ae phoned or someten

Give the guy a break Mhari, ma Da goes.

I didnae know yer number, he had a pure riddy.

Danny wis just sayin how he liked yer drawins.

Ma Da hung ma drawins aw over the hoose. He bought the frames oot the charity shop an framed them hisel. Most ae the wans in the livin room wer ae local places, street scenes ae the toon an that. At first when he found the portraits I did ae ma Ma he framed them an hung them up as well. Then wan day I came home from school an they wernae hangin up any more. I came across them wan time in his bedroom cupboard. He had them aw wrapped up in newspaper. Ye used tae bable tae make oot the marks wher they'd been hangin on the livin room wall. Till he put up other drawins tae hide the empty spaces.

Dae ye want tae come intae ma room tae I dry ma hair? I asks Danny.

Aye, he says.

Is it aw right Da? I says tae give him his place.

Aye, away ye's go, ma Da says. Ye don't want tae be hangin aboot wi an old dude like me.

I got Danny tae grab the hall mirror aff the wall an carry it intae ma bedroom. He sat on the bed an I plugged in ma hairdryer an sat on the floor. We tritae talk but I had tae keep switchin aff the hairdryer. Ended up he picked ma sketchbook up aff the floor an started lookin through it. I wis watchin him in the mirror as he flicked over the pages an I tritae work oot what drawin he wis lookin at. He stopped at wan page an wis starin at it for ages. I didnae know what sketch it wis an ma arse wis makin buttons. I wis aboot tae switch aff the hairdryer an ask him what he wis lookin at when he turned over the page.

Wance I finished dryin ma hair I didnae know if I should sit on the bed next tae Danny or else pull ma chair oot from ma wee foldy-up table I use for drawin. Ended up I just stayed wher I wis on the floor. He wis sittin on the bed wi the sketchpad open in front ae him. None ae us says anythin an he kept turnin the pages.

The teacher wis talkin the day aboot how hard it's gonnae be tae get intae art school, I eventually says.

What's yer chances? he asks, shuttin the pad.

Just as well he never says nothin aboot ma sketches. I hate it when people that arenae intae drawin tritae make comments. Even if ther positive, sayin stuff like, it's good, or else, I like yer drawin. Though what pisses me aff even worse is if somedae thinks they know someten aboot drawin an they tritae be dead fancy. I member I entered a competition wance. I never won nothin. But wan ae the judges wrote, Her city streets suggest a potential menace as they recede into shadow. I'm tellin ye I didnae have a clue what he wis on aboot.

It's hard tae tell, I says. I need tae bone up on ma english. But mostly I need tae concentrate on drawin figures.

Figures, he says. That's people intit?

Aye, I says.

Well I'm nae good at english, he goes. But if yer lookin for somedae tae draw I'd be more than happy tae help.

Wance I thought aboot it Danny seemed like the kind ae person I wouldnae feel so self-conscious drawin. He wis totally laid back, the kind ae guy ye felt comfortable roon aboot. Mibbe it wis someten tae dae wi his smokin hash but he had wan ae they far away looks aboot him. The more I thought ae it the more it began tae seem like a good idea.

I mibbe take ye up on that, I says, gettin up aff the floor an sittin next tae him on the bed.

Anytime, he says.

So did ye enjoy yersel on Saturday nite? I asks.

Aye, it wis good wintit.

Aye, I says.

We started winchin an I lay back on the bed an pulled him on top ae me. He wis a good kisser an didnae tritae feel me up. After a bit we broke aff an wer lyin on top ae the bed facin each other.

Isit aw right tae skin up? he asks.

Aye, I says. I wis a bit hesitant cause ae ma Da but I didnae want Danny tae think I wis a daft wee lassie. Ma Da used tae smoke dope when he wis on the drink but no anymore. Though I knew for a fact he'd bable tae smell it.

We don't have tae smoke it in here, Danny says.

It'll be awright, I says, gettin up aff the bed an shovin the towel at the bottom ae the door an openin ma bedroom window.

Danny built the joint an I raked through ma CD's. I felt dead self-conscious aboot what tae pick but ended up I settled for *Glasvegas*. If he didnae like it then it wis his problem. Wance I put the disc in he handed me the joint tae light. I stood up at the window an had a puff an wance I passed it tae him he done the same.

I'd smoked dope before in ma bedroom when ma Da wisnae in, but that wis wi Janie. It's much better when yer wi a bhoy an ye've got a wee bit ae a vibe goin on. I wis checkin oot his arse as he leaned oot the room window an at wan point he started singin tae hisel. I hit the giggles an he took a pure riddy but he soon got over it an we ended up laughin our heids aff. Wance we heard ma Da goin tae the toilet that soon stopped our gigglin.

Dae ye want a cup ae tea? I asks.

I don't think I finished that cup yer Da made me, he goes.

Aw the more reason tae have another wan, I goes.

I went intae the kitchen an filled the kettle. Ma Da came oot ae the bathroom an I asks him if he wanted a cup ae tea. He came intae the kitchen wi a big grin on his face.

Things goin awright? he asks.

Aye Da, I says, tritae avoid eye contact. I like him.

Good, wis aw he says.

Dae ye want a cup? I asks.

Aye, thanks, he says. By the way ye left this in the toilet, he reached intae his housecoat pocket an pulled oot ma mobile.

I had three missed calls from Janie.

Me an Danny spent the rest ae the nite listenin tae music an sittin on top ae the bed winchin. He didnae make another joint an he didnae tritae feel me. I kept lookin at his face an thinkin aboot how I'd mibbe draw him. I mean he wis a good lookin guy, but no in a pretty-boy way.

Dear Madam

Lindsay Macgregor

Thank you for your letter postmarked
yesterday in which you leave so much
unwritten – I can read between

the lines. I know you know I'd notice
how your vowels press so closely
to your consonants. And your use

of exclamation marks speaks to me
of something beyond irony – dare I suggest
desire for intimacy? When you propose

a visit, you make it sound illicit
with that carefully eroticised ellipsis...
And I suspect the casual nature

of your valediction is a little insincere –
you avoid the use of 'love' no doubt
in case you put me off. But I'm still here...

Frank

Claire Askew

is quiet at his window,
cut to ribbons by his Double Two shirt,
the slices of the old blind,
sunlight jutting in.
He's often there, watching the year
assert itself: magpies lining their smart black coats
with light, daffodils setting up camp.

Captain Frank, retired, is 84.
He has no car, no dog
and no TV, but lives
the tiny dramas of the street.
It's Frank who sugars grit along the path
before the snowfall comes.
It's Frank who takes in everybody's bins.

I looked up once from stacking wood
and found him at the front gate
with a gift for me: two ancient, dark red bricks.
A storm is on its way, he said.
Tie everything down.

All day I watch Frank's house – identical
to mine – but no one comes or goes.
All day I wear the same stripe back
and forth across the pale straw rug.

Frank stands and tracks the movement
of the crows, the local dogs, the bin man's truck.
Beyond the street the yards are full of fitted sheets
inflating on their whirligigs.

At night the wind plays sad trombones
under the eaves. I have the same recurring dream:
the houses shed their blotchy pebbledash
and blow away like paper lamps.
All except for mine and Frank's.

Directions for burial

Claire Askew

The beech woods are no good for hiding bodies:
shallow root pans fan out wide like pipes,
so only moss grows on the dappled bones.

The dead are better off set into patios,
the floors of sheds – better put to bed
in the cemetery's simple cots.

If you have lots to dispose of,
then bulldoze a pit. Doesn't every thing
rot down in time? Earth's skin is thick –

tilled with shrapnel and buckshot,
unexploded shells ploughed in like raisins
through a cake – the earth can take it.

So bring your loved one in their varnished box,
or the stretchers bearing strangers from the blast;
bring the child slung on your shoulder like a sack of rice.

Bring the parts you can't identify in garbage bags.
Bring the weapons used – the black box and the fuselage,
the parachutes that clammed and tangled –
lower them into the earth's dark mouth.
And what about the run-off and the holding pool?
The groundwater will take that too.

For hot exhaust and bitumen, the ocean will.
The ocean's building islands out of soda cans and plastic tubs,
industrious: ghostly tugs the gulls follow around.

Row out and cast your net for treasure no one wants.
Dig down just about anywhere and plunder gold: old rope,
an iron fence bombed flat, a mantrap, shotgun, landing gear.
The thing we fear: the day earth pulls its teeth out one by one,
when every landmine comes up like a bulb,
and all the seeds we've planted furiously bloom.

Posthuman Jungian Analysis

Lindsay Macgregor

Posthuman Jungian Analysis
And then, when I had nothing more
to say to her, a crow
alighted on the neighbour's chimney pot,
cawed its warning note,
and took off for the Tay, in tatters.

She asked me what the matter was,
insisted that there's no distinction
between the thinker and
what's thought about.

I couldn't disagree but knew
that crow did not belong to me.

Balance O Pooer

Donald Adamson

Hivvin for ae day
the shamanistic gift
o craw-leid
Ah cam upon him,
a stuffie, beaky chiel.

He luikit strecht in ma een
and Ah kent his thocht:
'Wi oor wings and birsin beaks
if we hid airms and haunds
we'd feenish ye.'

Ah sweir he cam efter me
aa the wey doon the wuid,
ilka thocht like a nieve.
Ah wis rinnin the gauntlet o him
tree bi tree.

Black Bull

Leonie M Dunlop

Heid cooried intae Silurian Greywackes,
black an short haired
wi whelks ticht oan its flanks.
It snorts agin the rocks,
nostrils bellowing auld fires.
Its hooves struck intae the noo cauld furnace,
haunches pushing intae the foundatiouns of land and seabed
while the waves birl at its hochs.

The Geologist and the Ox of Siccar Point

Leonie M Dunlop

Red Ox,
pulling with the strain of three million years,
furrowing folds into Devonian Red Sandstone,
chest sweating with wash from the ocean
as it stretches rock into runrigs.

The ox treads the Silurian Greywackes,
squelching up to its fetlocks in the soft rock,
holding open a gap in time.
The stone begins to harden.

Yoked to the harness of the grey stone below,
Red Ox created Hutton's crumbling tower
of curved folds on narrow furrows:
'a beautiful picture of this junction washed bare by the sea.'
A Neptunist's triumph broadcast.

Thochts on Hugh

George T Watt

Atap Ben Dorian luikin doun on Loch Tulla
I saw the watergaw,
'yon antrin thing' an thocht on ye.

The edges of the lochan wir blurred
an Glen Orchy wavered in the misty apparition,
ma een deceivit normality,
like yersel a spectre, unconveintional, flichty,
but aye colorfu, flummoxed an bambazed.

I luikit ower the range tae aa pynts o the compass,
arrayed afore me a muckle vista o sic wunners,
I wis mare than hummelt, I wis cocooned,
closeted in a timelessness ayont the thocht o ony man,
a consciensness o nationhuid,
as colorfu, indistinct an tantalisin
as yon watergaw.

Blow

Jim Carruth

How often fate chooses the best of the herd to fail
so that morning he is on the phone to the practice
hoping his description alone will provide a diagnosis
and a cure without the costliness of a consultation.

The growth looks like the bubbles in new milk froth.
No, more like the dark reddish lump of haematite
I've seen in a display cabinet at the village museum.
That's not right either, doesn't capture the extent of it.

He reaches to make it real, remembers the vet's last visit:
Count Basie's big band blasting out from his battered Austin.
Picture Dizzy's puffed up cheeks as his lips are pressed hard
to the mouthpiece of the horn – the swelling's exactly that.

Schoolmates

Jim Carruth

The longest walks are the ones trudged
through early years and winter months
slow miles from farmyard to the iron gates
the worst of all weathers in heavy boots,
working clothes more suited for the field
to arrive late behind the calling of the bell.
There to learn from the discipline of the strap
that when words are clumsy on the tongue
and your rough hands have struggled all day
to line them up in the right order on the page
while all around you the neat use laughter
as a weapon, best choose a hunter's silence
a schooling of sorts between useful chores.

Lost Orchard

Jim Carruth

I stand at the bend on Broadway at East 10th Street
My silence marks an absence, yellow cabs hoot at me
on this curve made around an apple orchard long gone.
A blanket of horn blasts are no shroud for a resurrection
though I listen hard to a lost voice rustle in the breeze.
I did not climb among its leaves, was not there to see
and hear ripe fruit drop to the ground in Autumn sun
but in my life I've savoured other apples on my tongue
and as long as I recall the joy of tasting just the one
its weight, shine of skin, juice sweet or sour sharp
how could I ever swing my axe at any stranger's bark.

The city agreed in 1815 to bend Broadway at Mr. Brevoort's farm, at East 10th Street, where the street still curves today.

Before he could think or change his mind, he tucked the hand inside the elasticated waistband of his pyjama pants, and knotted the cord of his bathrobe tightly over the wrist. He could feel the cool palm and soft fingers resting against the skin of his stomach but it didn't feel bad.

What Remains
Vicki Jarrett

What Remains

from the collection The Way Out

Vicki Jarrett

Standing by the sink in his kitchen, Marvin ran his hand under the cold tap until his finger bones ached like the roots of bad teeth. Was this to be the next thing then? Reduced to making tepid cups of tea to save himself from injury at his own shaking hand. He dabbed it dry with a cloth and examined the damage. There was a red scald the shape of Africa on the back of his left hand and it was beginning to hurt.

He looked out at the other houses lit in a golden haze from the streetlights. In the small upstairs bedroom of the house opposite, the pacing silhouette of a woman with a baby circled in the muted yellow light, round and round, like a sleepy goldfish. He pushed the window open a crack and listened to the child's cries rising and falling; a tiny human siren protesting the night.

Some days Marvin passed the mother in the street, her hair unwashed, narrow shoulders hunched. She looked like the stroller was the only thing holding her up. He'd offered to help her with her groceries once but she'd looked at him as if he'd volunteered to tap dance naked, and hurried into her house. Perhaps she didn't speak English. Considering how rarely folks around here spoke to each other these days, for all he knew they could each be speaking their own private languages.

Marvin didn't sleep a whole lot anymore. The small hours often found him in the kitchen, making tea to take back to bed. He still lay on the left hand side. The right retained Kath's shape, and although she hadn't filled it for over a decade now, when he woke with the scent of her around his face, the taste of her on his lips, he would reach into the empty space and find her gone all over again. After forty years together, what was left now but to miss her?

There was no point going back to the States. There was nothing there for him anymore, not even a decent cup of tea. At least here he could feel he was still with Kath, surrounded by what remained. This house. These memories. She used to joke he was her war bride. Instead of the pair of them shipping off to the States when they'd married after the war, she'd convinced him to make the move to her side of the Atlantic. Not that he'd put up much of a fight. He'd have moved to Timbuktu if that was what she'd wanted. They'd had a good life together. Children hadn't come along, which was a sadness, but they'd always had each other.

Sometimes the lack was like a great ragged hole in his guts, other times it was worse. He hadn't believed he could miss her more until yesterday when, for a whole horrifying minute, he had completely forgotten her name.

The memory gaps were happening more often now. At least he thought they were, but how could he know for sure? He shook his head as he set the kettle to boil again. Stood to reason, if he could recall that his memory was bad, then it couldn't be so bad as all that. It was a little patchy, that was all. No big deal.

He sat at the kitchen table with a fresh cup of tea and picked up the envelope from the Council. It contained details of the home help they were sending to his house. He'd told them he didn't need any help, thank you kindly. Didn't want some do-gooder poking around his kitchen, prying in his fridge, handling things. He could manage just fine.

When the gas main exploded under number 36 flinging slates, bricks and assorted debris high into the night sky, winking across the stars to land in the back gardens and hedges of neighbouring houses, Marvin looked up.

On the heels of the initial boom of the explosion, the low growl and crackle of fire breathed through his open window. He got up from the table, walked towards the window and blinked slowly. Perhaps the street would be back to normal when he opened his eyes, but when he did, he found himself looking straight into the face of the woman across the street. Both her and the baby were staring straight back at him, framed in their window, while fire splashed lurid orange light over the houses.

Lights were going on up and down the street now. People were emerging, bewildered in their nightclothes, stumbling over slippers; drawn towards the fire, they still looked to each other and raised their hands to their mouths, hoping someone else would know what to do. Marvin pulled on his bathrobe and went outside. The crowd milled and clustered, and stepped over the smouldering remnants of exploded house strewn around the street. He was standing at the edge of the crowd when he felt a tug at his sleeve. The baby giggled and tugged again, his chubby hand clasped a handful of Marvin's bathrobe while his mother was busy talking to a woman with long grey braids wearing a Mickey Mouse t-shirt. Marvin held out a finger and the baby grasped and pulled it towards his mouth.

'Hungry are you, buddy?' he asked the baby conspiratorially. 'That what keeps you up at night?' At the sound of his voice, the mother turned her head towards him and narrowed her eyes. 'I always see your light on,' Marvin smiled. She didn't respond. 'Your bedroom light,' he said, wondering again if she spoke English. She raised her eyebrows and drew her baby towards her. 'Not that I'm watching you or anything,' Marvin raised his hands in a gesture of reassurance. 'Nothing like that.' As the woman backed away to the other side of the crowd, he heard the lonely howl of approaching sirens, drawing closer.

The fire engines blasted into the street, a controlled explosion of red paint and blue lights, scattering the residents before them. Firefighters jumped out wearing dayglo jackets and helmets with visors. The police arrived and set about crowd control.

'Move back, please. For your own protection. Stay back.' A kid in uniform herded them across the street, away from the burning building. 'Sorry,' he told them, 'you can't return to your homes just yet but if you'll be patient, we'll let you know as soon as it's safe.'

Finding himself entangled in the docile shuffling of the crowd, Marvin fought his way clear. There must be something he could do to help. Where were the couple that had lived at number 36? Perhaps they were wandering around somewhere dazed and lost, disoriented from the shock, or injured so badly they couldn't move or call out. Someone should be trying to find them. He set off, looking into gardens, around sheds and behind bushes. The cold air poked chill fingers into the folds of his bathrobe and he realised with a familiar dismay that he needed to go, and soon. It was bad enough at his age without the cold, and it sure wasn't helping. He glanced around. He needed to find somewhere quickly.

Marvin edged around a box hedge into a deserted front garden and found a good dark corner. As he stood there, sighing with relief, he looked up at the smoke drifting past the stars. The folks from number thirty-six had likely been blown up and burnt during the explosion and could even be floating by, within those clouds.

He was just finishing off when he heard a noise behind him. Startled, he spun round and came face to face with a thin, young woman with lank hair, holding a baby. There was something familiar about her. She looked at him and her eyes dropped to his crotch where his hand still flapped and jerked as he attempted to tidy himself back into his pyjama pants.

Her eyes widened in shock for a second then narrowed and her mouth twisted sideways. She pushed a breath out through her nose and turned away. Marvin understood well enough what she meant.

'No. It isn't...I wasn't...It's a tremor...'

Marvin tried to explain but she was already gone. He started to follow and his foot came down on something soft. Oh crap. Please, not dog shit on my slippers, he thought. He looked down and gently lifted his foot.

There on the garden path was a human hand, lying palm up, open, like a strange pale flower in the dark. It had been severed at the wrist but was otherwise intact. By the size of it, and the rings, he could tell it was a woman's hand, must be Mrs thirty-six's. It was her left hand, Marvin noted. He felt a little dizzy as he stood staring at it, wondering what he should do. The ring finger bore an engagement ring and a wedding band, grown slightly too tight over the years and digging into the flesh, the same way Kath's rings had. He remembered the way her hands had lain open on the bedspread, pleading for relief, even as the warmth left her body. And there had been nothing, not one goddamned thing, he could do for her.

Maybe he should pick the hand up but he didn't want to touch it. In any case, he reasoned, you weren't supposed to move a body so probably you shouldn't move pieces of them either. He went to the edge of the garden and looked around, hoping to find someone official nearby, but there was no one. He could see the fire was being brought under control, the flames sinking lower behind the black shadow-puppet silhouettes of his neighbours.

Perhaps he should call for help. He cleared his throat. 'Help?' he tried, but his voice sounded thin and papery. 'Help!' he tried again, but the word jammed in his throat and crushed itself, like it was too big to get out.

As Marvin debated the matter, the hand lay passively on the ground, the fingers curled inwards slightly, lines on the palm picked out by the fading orange light. As he gazed at it, he felt strangely peaceful. Like the scent of some macabre night-blooming flower, the hand released a hypnotic innocence, a frank helplessness that both charmed and troubled him.

Time passed.

The yapping of a dog brought Marvin out of his trance. A small tan-coloured terrier was in the garden, padding eagerly towards the hand. Marvin stepped between the hand and the dog. The dog stopped and looked at Marvin with its head cocked to one side for a second but then continued on, trotting around him towards the hand, its pink tongue poking out over white teeth. Marvin put himself between the two again and, before he thought it all the way through, he growled, low and threatening and finished with a sharp warning bark and a step forwards. The dog whimpered and backed off out of the garden, then bolted off up the street. Marvin allowed himself a small smile. Not such a helpless old coot after all.

The hand was still there. He'd have to pick it up. That was the only thing to do. He'd pick it up and take it to somebody official and they could deal with it.

The wrist end was seared like a Sunday roast. He bent down and grasped the hand firmly by the wrist. It lolled slightly as he lifted it. It wasn't stiff yet and although it was cool to the touch, it still felt human, real.

He walked to the edge of the path and hesitated. The whole street was outside, including women and children. He couldn't just go wandering around with a severed hand in plain sight. He stepped back into the garden and tried putting it in the pocket of his bathrobe but whichever way he put it in, the other end stuck out and would be clearly visible. Then he had an idea.

Before he could think or change his mind, he tucked the hand inside the elasticated waistband of his pyjama pants, and knotted the cord of his bathrobe tightly over the wrist. He could feel the cool palm and soft fingers resting against the skin of his stomach but it didn't feel bad. The hand was good and secure and wouldn't be upsetting anyone there.

Marvin left the garden and walked back towards the dying fire. All he had to do was find someone in a uniform and explain the situation. Simple.

He was only a few steps away from the crowd when he felt the hand begin to slip. He slowed to a shuffle and tightened the cord on his bathrobe again. But it was too late. Just as he reached the crowd it skidded down further, then stopped. Had things been just a little different, thought Marvin, if a few specific details could've been adjusted, a woman's hand down there would have been welcome.

His shoulders slumped as he looked at the firemen, continuing to pour gallons of water onto the blackened, smoking ruins of number 36. People were bustling about being efficient with clipboards. 'You can go back to your homes now,' a voice announced, 'The gas is off so it's perfectly safe. If you could all clear the area.'

Marvin didn't move. He was worried the hand would slip again, drop down the leg of his pyjama pants and out the other end. The other residents started to drift away in ones and twos, back to their own homes. One of the firemen was looking at Marvin.

'Alright there, mate?' he asked, 'You lost?'

'Um, no, not exactly,' muttered Marvin. He wanted to tell them, but the prospect of fishing the hand from inside his pyjama pants in the middle of the street seemed like a very bad idea.

This wasn't the way he'd imagined things would work out. The ambulance doors slammed and the driver switched the lights off and started the engine. They must have the rest of what was left of the couple from number 36 in there. Perhaps he could run after them, tell them they'd dropped a bit. But before he could form a plan, the ambulance was driving out of the street.

'Are you sure you're okay?' asked the fireman. Marvin nodded, although he wasn't sure, not sure at all. 'You can go home now. Get some rest.' He patted Marvin on the shoulder and moved back to the business of clearing up. Marvin turned and walked, very slowly, back to his house.

Climbing the step to his kitchen door forced him to lift his feet above the low shuffle that had got him this far. The movement dislodged the hand and it skidded down his leg, trailing fingernails down his thigh, fumbling over his kneecap and finally flopping out from the cuff of his pant leg and onto the floor with a slap. He stooped to pick it up, closed the door behind him and gazed around the room. He felt an obligation to the hand now, to protect it and see that it came to no harm. He would figure out what to do later. For now he laid the hand on the bottom shelf of the fridge and closed the door.

He went to the sink, poured a cold cup of tea down the plug hole and set the kettle to boil. This was happening more often lately. It felt like he was forever making tea but hardly ever got to drink any. Through the window, he watched the morning dissolve the remains of the night while the wall clock ticked off another new start.

Marvin sniffed. There was a strong smell of burning. He checked the toaster, the hob and the oven. Sometimes he forgot things so it was best to check. He didn't want to wind up burning the house down. He sat at the table and picked up the letter from the Council, pausing to inspect a red mark on the back of his left hand. It was roughly the shape of India. How had that happened?

There was a banging sound. He listened to it for a while before he realised someone was knocking at his front door. The knocking came again, louder this time. He opened the door. The woman on the doorstep beamed at him, grasped his hand and pumped it up and down.

'You'll be Marvin,' she shouted. And before he could either agree or disagree, she was in his house, bustling down the hall towards the kitchen. 'I'm Judith,' she said, 'the home help? Remember?' She laughed. 'Don't you worry, Marvin, we'll get you sorted out.' She began unpacking a supermarket bag, laying bread, butter, tea and milk out on the worktop. 'I've brought you a few basics. Let's start with a nice cup of tea. Would you like a cup of tea, Marvin?'

The Chilean Way

Extract from the novel Once a Great Leader

Rodge Glass

It's 1970.

After being nominated as a candidate for President of Chile, the nation's great poet Pablo Neruda[1] pulls out of the race early on, stepping aside to allow his friend Salvador Allende to stand unopposed as the leader of the Unidad Popular.[2] This coalition comprises communists, socialists and most of the country's left wing parties, and it has a real chance of a breakthrough, but Allende, a Marxist, has suffered repeated near misses at the ballot box and the pre-election signs aren't clear – so there's no champagne waiting to spill its cork. He jokes his gravestone will read: 'Here lies Salvador Allende, Future President of Chile'. But this time he surprises many, including himself, by emerging victorious, and Neruda notes drily, among friends, that 'Salvador will need a different epitaph now.'

Still, the result is tight. On September 4th 1970 he gains just 36.2% of the vote, with his nearest challenger ex-President Ruben Allessandri[3] on 34.9% – but majorities are rare in Chile, and a win is a win. After the traditional seven week hiatus – nothing happens quickly on this continent – the senate finally ratifies Allende, and this makes him the first ever democratically elected Marxist President on earth, pricking up ears worldwide at a time when the Cold War is at its height. At his inauguration, Allende talks about 'The Chilean Way', meaning the kind of democratic socialism he believes can be forged in his back yard then exported to the world, no blood shed. But the Chilean Way is a route fraught with obstacles, not least those which link the new administration to Cuba. Fidel Castro calls Allende *compañero,* which can be translated as 'comrade'. His own revolution is perceived as a threat to the West, and all of Latin and Central America is on alert. To Allende, it feels like the whole world is.[4]

---

1 Pablo Neruda (1904 – 1973), born Neftali Ricardo Reyes Basoalto), the Nobel Prize winning poet and communist Chilean diplomat who had homes in Santiago, Valparaiso and Isla Negra, now all museums. Though originally made famous by his *Twenty Love Poems and a Song of Despair* in the 1920s, Neruda became one of the most recognisable and popular figures in Chilean history, a legend in his time. Neruda did serve briefly as a Senator, but afterwards confined his political statements to his work. Died several weeks after the coup of 11th September 1973, his home ransacked by the military. Broken-hearted in his final days, turned into a hate figure by Pinochet's regime, Neruda remains not just a national hero but an international one.

2 Some commentators believe Neruda was never serious about standing for President. Though a popular figure he was also deeply divisive, and for Neruda, political poetry came before poetic politics. When asked if he would really take on the job Neruda famously answered, 'Perhaps. But my afternoon nap is non-negotiable.' After Allende's victory he made Neruda Chilean Ambassador to France, a job he carried out until 1972, when his health began to fail.

3 Ruben Allessandri (1896-1986) was the 27th President of Chile, a conservative who was in office from 1958-1964. Son of Arturo Allessandri, President of Chile from 1920-1925 and 1932-1938. Part of the so-called 'Chilean elite', the unofficial members club which had run the country for decades.

4 The relationship between these two Socialist bulwarks was not all mutual agreement. Castro made a mixed three week trip to Chile later in Allende's reign, where he publicly denounced some of his comrade's policies, on Chilean soil, in front of the man himself. They disagreed on method, also violence. Meanwhile Allende's team felt Castro stayed too long and expected too much. He was not treated like a God in Chile, and couldn't understand why.

In the White House, fingers are twitching. President Richard Nixon and his Secretary of State Henry Kissinger, who have already been financing the Chilean opposition to the tune of millions of dollars, react to Allende's election by upping their efforts to 'get rid of him'. It's understood what that phrase means. Nixon cuts off funding to the new Chilean government, cancelling all lending to Chilean companies. He bombs power lines and negotiates in secret with anti-government forces. In the face of such weighty opposition, little Chile is quickly isolated in the international arena. Though neither would admit it, Nixon and Kissinger become fixated during this period, fearing that if they don't deal swiftly and strongly with the situation then Chile might become another Vietnam. But rather than send troops south to bring down Allende, something which would not have been tolerated by the US public (the *real* Vietnam War is of course still limping on, leaving all sides tired and confused), the White House prefers to use these multiple spoiling tactics, which amount to one thing: sabotage.[5]

At home, confidence in the new Chilean government is fragile. The President's enemies are everywhere. Inflation is already climbing and, though economics is not Allende's strong suit, he's planning to nationalize many of Chile's resources, much to the displeasure of international companies profiting from the current system, also upsetting the established Chilean elite. The army, navy and air force are a fat slice of that elite and they're uneasy too, with much division between those who believe their allegiance is to the President, 'whoever that mongrel may be', and those who say Allende represents a threat to the state which they are duty bound to eliminate. Meanwhile, though he later denies it in his memoirs[6], an unremarkable army man of limited intelligence called Augusto Pinochet benefits from Allende's regime, gaining promotions by keeping his head down and licking the boots of his superiors. As the temperature skyrockets in government, the men above him are dropping fast.[7] Few notice the General's swift rise.

None of this is felt directly in Cabo Pasado, a tiny pueblo in the heart of the mid-northern Valle de Elqui region where a child is about to be born into the Moya family. However, there is definitely something in the air. People wonder what the new government will lead to. They look at each other differently in the street, thinking, are you one of us? And if not, then who are you? Regardless of allegiance, everyone notices certain things. In the last few weeks, the price of bread has gone up several times.

---

5 The release of confidential files in the year 2000 from the Nixon era reveal that the United States regularly and heavily funded right-wing candidates in successive Chilean elections. They also revealed the USA's direct involvement in the overthrow of Allende in the military coup of 1973, and their active involvement in Pinochet's Chile afterwards. Despite what Kissinger writes in his memoirs (*Years of Upheaval*, Little, Brown, 1982), all this was conducted with the full knowledge of the human rights abuses being conducted under the US-backed military junta which succeeded Allende.

6 This refers to *Memoirs of a Soldier*, by General Augusto Pinochet (Talleres Graficos del Instituto Geografico Militar: Santiago, 1990), though Pinochet also covered similar material in his memoir of the coup itself, *The Decisive Day* (Estado Mayor General del Ejercito, Santiago, 1982)

7 According to Heraldo Muñoz's book *The Dictator's Shadow: Life Under Augusto Pinochet*, Pinochet claimed that on the day Allende was elected, he announced to a room full of military subordinates that this development was a trajedy for Chile. He also vowed to bring Allende down. Overwhelming evidence backs up Muñoz's claim that this was entirely fabrication. Pinochet rose through the ranks by being loud to those below him and silent to those above.

María Moya Tejada was nineteen on her wedding day, and twenty when she fell pregnant. Before, during and after she got married she lived in her childhood bedroom at Casa Moya[8], the oldest and largest house in Cabo Pasado, where the family had been for five generations. She grew up in this room, with her two older sisters Daniela and Valentina, until they both got married two years earlier, within weeks of each other. For a spell she had the space to herself, enjoying the relative peace as she looked out from her window, nightly, dreamily, over sleepy little Cabo Pasado – they were a magical few months. Now she shared the room with her husband Gustavo Moya Cortez (no relation). Their lovemaking always had to be quiet, but that made it no less passionate.

Gustavo had been embraced by María's parents as if he was their own. The son of a miner from the north who had retired to the Valle de Elqui after an accident on site, Gustavo had partially raised himself, and the Moyas had known him since he was a child. A wanderer who liked to walk aimlessly around the village waving to familiar faces, he was a boy the family had nicknamed 'El Chico Gentil', the gentle boy, or the friendly boy. He seemed only capable of seeing the good in others, even if they were about to betray him. It was said of Gustavo that he would smile at the devil, even one wielding a knife and bracing for the plunge. But as María's father Ruben reminded him when he visited Casa Moya to ask for her hand, goodness feeds no-one. As he could not yet hope to provide for María, the conditions of marriage were clear: Gustavo and María would live in Casa Moya until they could afford independence. If that day never came, then so be it, they would never leave. But neither would they starve.

María's mother Alejandra was a constant presence throughout the pregnancy, a steady, quiet support. Ruben was there daily too. He was a fisherman who marked his return to the household in the same way most nights, by slapping the day's bounty on the table. 'Bueno,' he would say, announcing himself with that first word, loud enough for the whole house to hear. 'The Moyas defeat the sea once more!' He had to come home with full hands. As well as Ruben, Alejandra, María and now Gustavo, María's sisters and their husbands Oscar and Eduardo also regularly came to stay at Casa Moya, as well as two (alas, unnamed) cousins who slept on the floor in the summer season, and Alejandra's elderly sister (also called María), who came to stay at weekends. María Moya Senior was a woman who was famous for hurling insults at the young ones and demanding, as 'the most senior living Moya', to sit at the head of the table.

Outside the house there was plenty happening too – Ruben's horse, three pigs, two cows and barn full of chickens were the noisiest part of an already noisy family. So Casa Moya was full, the walls buzzed morning and night, and there was always a meal being

---

8 Casa Moya had always been known by this name, for as long as anyone in the village could remember. But it took on a double meaning when María Moya Tejada married her schoolfriend Gustavo Moya Cortez in May 1969. The two families were, as far as anyone could identify, unrelated, but it did make for joke in the local community, as well as somewhat complicating the family's identity at a crucial time. Given the Latin American tradition of children carrying both their parents' surnames for a single generation, this might technically, potentially, have made the future Prime Minister of Britain Gabriela Emilia Moya Moya – but all parties concerned agreed this was ridiculous, and the second 'Moya' was dropped.

eaten or about to be. Casa Moya overlooked the Rio Pasado (meaning the tranquil, or the peaceful river). It was perched on the top of a small hill in the middle of town, and could be seen from many other homes, giving it a fine view of the water. The continual hum of the place was electricity to those quieter homes surrounding it, and all that happened there was soon known everywhere, the slightest rumour seized upon as fact by superstitious locals, so swiftly in fact that it seemed like these rumours were being carried by the cool wind of the valley, from Casa Moya and down to the village below, then down further, to the sandy track where the pueblo shuffled to an end and the trickle of the Rio Pasado began. In that spot, as Alejandra often said to María, all rumours, true and untrue, began their last journey, floating away along with the leaves, and twigs, and marine life. *Se fue*, gone, forever, as if they'd never existed.

In those days, the people of Cabo Pasado lived mostly as if they were on a small island no-one had visited for many years, far from the city and so still that even the passing of an unknown car counted as news. (So no wonder the events at Casa Moya were such a regular source of conversation.) 1970 might have been a shaky year in Chilean history, with the political situation getting more volatile by the day – some said it was as if the great earthquake of 1968 was still going – but on most days it was as if the sea and mountainous cordillera surrounding the people of the valley allowed them to pretend events in metropolitan Chile didn't affect them, at least for now. How could they? The village was as tranquil as the river, the view of the mountains the same as last week, last year, last century. This might seem like a contradiction – to say Cabo Pasado was untouched by national events, though national events impacted upon it. If it seems like a contradiction, that's because it is. But as we shall see, such contradictions were typical of the area, of the country as a whole, and were understood as part of life in the Valle de Elqui, a place where myth and reality worked in tandem. On any day or any week, both opposites could be true.

*

Perhaps it needs an outsider to make sense of what was happening. Arturo Rodriguez, now the current Chilean Minister for Education, was then a local junior councilman in his early twenties, sent to the Valle de Elqui part of the Coquimbo region[9], for a year on secondment by his bosses in Chile's second-oldest city, La Serena. He visited Cabo Pasado regularly as part of his duties, and retains strong links with its people to this day, holidaying there every summer. When asked about this period, specifically about the atmosphere in 1970, he spoke in the mystical tone more typical of the locals:

---

9 This is also known as Region IV

Out in the valley, the mountains don't talk. Or they do, but you have to listen closely to hear them. And though we heard a little rumbling – we did get newspapers you know! – we chose not to listen to the sound. If you'd asked me at the time what life was like in Cabo Pasado, I would have told you: *Nothing happens here. It never will.* The events of the next few months proved otherwise. And I was as guilty as anyone for ignoring the sounds the mountains were making. Looking back, I realize now, it was as if they were waving their hands, and crying out.[10]

Though Rodriguez was beginning to feel local, he was really a city boy, and several decades younger than the average age in Cabo Pasado, having been sent there by his father – who got him a job in the locality through connections that would eventually save his life.[11] Most people in Cabo Pasado didn't have such luxuries. Men sat on their steps because there was little work, they shrank in number each year, and many of these remaining villagers were counting down their last years. Though it claimed to be working for the emancipation of just these sorts of people, some of the most elderly and vulnerable feared the new government, the threat of its collapse, what might follow. Meanwhile, the prospect of a newborn in the Moya household filled them up inside; there had been no new arrivals in this little hamlet since just before 1968's terrible, famous shaking (the *terramodo*, or earthquake) which had destroyed the flimsy infrastructure of Cabo Pasado as well as so many other similar Chilean *pueblos* built with only short term survival in mind. 'When God shakes the tree,' Alejandra Moya had said, 'all the leaves can do is hold on for dear life and hope He'll soon get bored.' And they had held on. Life had seemed slower since the earthquake. Though unspoken, everyone knew this to be a truth. The birth of the brand new Moya to come gave people something to talk about which had the power to make them smile.

Around the time María Moya's pregnancy became undeniable, Gustavo Moya Cortez visited some friends. As there was no bar or restaurant in the village in those days, and locals wouldn't have been able to afford such a thing anyway, they often sat outside each other's homes and drank Pisco Sours while looking up at the stars.[12] (For those unfamiliar with the properties of this notorious drink, it's worth noting here that even a couple of Piscos can lead

---

10 Interview with ZMH, xx/xx/xx

11 Though arrested as a suspected communist in the early days of the Military Junta, Rodriguez's father managed to secure his son's release by calling in a favour with an old friend in charge of the prison where Arturo was being held. He spent just three days in jail. After his release the whole family fled to Paris, where they remained in exile until 1990. After the end of Pinochet's regime, Arturo Rodriguez secured a minor position in government, from which he rose steadily in the following decades.

12 Pisco Sour is a tangy grape brandy cocktail which is hugely popular in Chile. The origin of Pisco is still a hotly debated issue, one aggravated by the renaming of the village of La Union in the Elqui Valley as Pisco Elqui by President Gabriel Gonzalez Videla in the mid 20th Century. Many Peruvians claim Pisco as their national drink, a source of pride which they trace back to the original vineyards introduced by the Spanish conquistadors in the 17th Century. Chileans claim they have popularised the drink, and produce Pisco of a higher quality. This has been a cause of considerable tension between the nations in recent years, and continues to be, with the European Commission officially acknowledging Peru as the drink's birthplace as recently as 2013, reigniting a row which refuses to die.

to a powerful unleashing of the imagination.) After a few drinks Gustavo announced, eyes on the skies, that he had been visited in a dream by a *fantasma* who told him the newborn to come was going to be a boy. A strong one! To make all Cabo Pasado proud! The men raised their glasses, toasted the child and promised to pray for it. They sang folk songs and embraced and Gustavo's friends, socialists to a man, forgot to whisper when they talked about the future. Before collapsing into bed that night the men told their wives about Gustavo's dream and the following day their wives told their friends, and news boomeranged across the valley and back, soon landing at the door of Casa Moya with a thump. When she learned of the dream from a neighbour, Alejandra said to her husband, 'Watch out, Gustavo is seeing things. This summer is going to get hot.' Ruben grunted and left the room. In family matters, his wife was usually right. But that didn't mean he wanted to listen.

Gustavo was not the only one hoping for a male heir.

A week later, in early October, Father Ignacio Ramiro reported from the pulpit (while Gustavo, María and the family sat in the pews) that he too had been visited in a dream by the voice of God, who had something to say about the Moyas. The voice gave him a clear message: the whole village must pray for a boy. This child was destined to, in the words of the priest, 'grow up to be a great leader of men', 'one of Chile's finest sons, famous both at home and abroad'. A newborn girl would also be a fine human being – kind, considerate, and a proud patriot, but not an icon. What could a girl hope for in this world, he asked, arms outstretched? A good husband, healthy children, not much more – but for boys, history awaits. When Father Ramiro reported that the voice also warned a girl child would never marry, María said she felt ill and asked to be excused from church. How had she suddenly found herself at the centre of the *pueblo*? And how could she retreat into the shadows? As she crouched down outside, looking for a safe space to catch her breath, Daniela whispered to Valentina, 'I hope she's vomiting his words onto the steps.' Valentina, the oldest of the three and a devout, serious girl of twenty-two, didn't answer. Though as opinionated as her sisters, she was learning the virtues of silence, with the aim of pleasing her husband Eduardo, a man with views so traditional when it came to gender roles that even the staunchest chauvinist might baulk upon hearing them.

Some parishioners doubted the likelihood of the Lord finding time to visit two people in the same Chilean village, and one so remote, even if one of them was a priest – but others took the two dreams as corroborative evidence. They had come so close together! And was Jesus himself not born into poverty, in an unknown venue? Had his arrival not been predicted? Had the people of Bethlehem not scoffed at the idea of something noteworthy taking place in their town, only to be proved spectacularly, earth-shatteringly wrong? So the pious of Cabo Pasado did as they were told, clasped their hands and wished, and as María reached five and six months pregnant, interest in the birth began to bubble. The village square, which was also the entrance to the church, became home to gifts of flowers, offered to the statue of the Virgin Mary which stood proudly at the church's entrance. For every prayer heading skywards, every hope in the hearts of the locals, María Moya felt the pressure in her intensify a fraction. One evening she told Daniela, 'The greatest blessing would be a bus to take us all away from here.' Daniela nodded, then put a finger to her lips. 'If anyone suspects you think that,' she answered, stroking her sister's palm, 'we'll all be eaten alive'.

In recent weeks the three sisters had spent most of each day together, telling stories and reminiscing about their childhoods while hidden away in their old shared bedroom, as if this would somehow erase the present which was busy wrenching itself into new shapes, unbidden.[13] In the hours after Father Ramiro's dream became public, Daniela, Valentina and María held onto each other more tightly, spoke more urgently, and poor Gustavo was banished from his marital bed, the room regressing into its former identity as home to the three sisters. *Do you remember the time when...?* they whispered, behind their hands. *And that other time, when we...?* Gustavo was downstairs, his brain buzzing, his ears awake. Through the thin ceiling, the young newlywed sometimes thought the laughter of the three sisters sounded like contagious music. This he recognized from previous occasions in recent weeks when it felt like he was about to catch some fantastic, fatal bug. But he also noticed that on this night, the night of Father Ramiro's announcement, the laughter was strangely desperate – a sound which, at a distance, might have been confused for crying.

Despite the attempts of the three sisters, nothing was going to keep reality away, and they could not bring themselves to laugh in the same way as before. As they talked, they heard Alejandra and Ruben arguing under their breath in their bedroom next door. They couldn't hear what it was about, but by dinnertime it was clear. After a meal conducted almost entirely in shouts and accusations, Ruben announced that there was to be no further discussion around the family table about politics. He would not have his family destroyed by it any more. Enough was enough! Gustavo ate while looking at his food. 'Papa, you can't stop anything,' he said. Though the least politically active in the household, Gustavo was always the most likely to disagree with his father-in-law in public. After this, the two men said not a single word to each other for several long, difficult days. Alejandra prayed hard for reconciliation. If they couldn't stick together during testing times like this then what use was having a family at all?

At the start of the seventh month of pregnancy, December 1970, a vigil began to be held outside Casa Moya. Letters of goodwill arrived. One day fifteen members of the local church arrived and spent all evening saying prayers and dancing. They returned the following day with makeshift tents. Seeing this from her window, María covered her mouth with her hand. In the following days she retreated to her bed, refusing all requests from fortune tellers and healers who offered their services. She even refused Father Ramiro, who hadn't

---

13 This period of unification for the three sisters was made possible by the fact that Daniela and Valentina's husbands had recently left Cabo Pasado for a few weeks, claiming they were looking for work. Years later it was discovered that both men had taken lovers in another pueblo, another two sisters in fact – but for now their absence wasn't questioned. Already tired of their marriages and missing their home, both Daniela and Valentina embraced the opportunity to return to Casa Moya. The pull of that household over all its inhabitants seems to have been unusually strong.

been turned away from anywhere in Cabo Pasado since the drought. When he arrived, he insisted on saying prayers by the pregnant woman's bedside in order to 'ensure that a great leader is born to the village'. But Daniela shooed him away, telling him the mother-to-be was experiencing 'women's issues which were not for the eyes of a priest', and that he should 'please respect the family's privacy'. He insisted one more time, and had to be locked out by Alejandra, who called out, 'See you in Church on Sunday – and not before!' while the priest kept pushing. It's not that Father Ramiro wasn't capable of listening – he couldn't even hear the request. *Fantasmas* on his shoulder were whispering, *Danger, Danger.* All other noises were muted.

Father Ramiro knew that no chances could be taken with the future of his community. This was the new world of the Unidad Popular, and new rules applied to its operation. He had heard of other dying villages, in Chile and beyond, where now no child went hungry, simply because a son of that place had become a known singer, or poet, or politician. Look at Neruda! Look at Mistral! The newspapers were full of it, places not so far away that traded on the association, no matter how flimsy that association was. In the wake of the earthquake which had crushed Cabo Pasado so recently, the kind Charles Darwin said reminded him of 'plates shifting on a broken pie crust'[14], Father Ramiro knew his mission. He was ready to carry it out. And determined not to get caught between the plates.

The third time he was turned away from Casa Moya, the third occasion in four days, rumours caught fire that the family were hiding María from view because she was gravely ill, much more than they were prepared to admit, and that the child was in danger. Like a government under siege, the Moyas refused to confirm or deny the allegations – which Gustavo now confirms 'may have been a mistake'. As one elderly villager put it to me, 'Starve the community of news and it will begin to sprout from the skies'. And so it was. The very next day, one young parishioner reported having a dream which contained a warning. The dream delivered the clear message that the child could die – though, conveniently enough, it did not say why or how this might happen. This message was delivered by an unidentified flying object which hovered in the sky above the valley, calling out its horrible predication. (The parishioner confirmed, under questioning, that the UFO lowered itself from the night sky onto the cordillera, landed in the village square then departed, leaving behind a small green alien, who gave the warning. The alien's name, apparently, was Juan.)

In his sermon that Sunday, though two members of the Moya family were notably absent, Father Ramiro found himself speaking to swelled aisles, and he urged his flock to redouble their prayers. Many said it was the most impassioned they had ever seen him – some even whispered that it was as if their timid local priest had become possessed. Later that same

---

14 Darwin travelled to Latin America in 1831 on the HMS Beagle II captained by Robert FitzRoy, on what is known as the ship's Second Voyage. Darwin mainly took geological notes but also zoological ones which helped him form his later theories of evolution. HMS Beagle II traversed Latin America, including the West coast of the continent, making stops in Chiloe, Valparaiso and Santiago amongst other places. Darwin had previously had little passion for geology but fell in love with it during this trip, and considered Chile's earthquakes to be some of the most notable experiences of his trip.

day, still swimming with energy, and with the charge of his parishioners throbbing in his bones, he penned a letter to his superiors in the capital: 'Our humble church's finances might be in a parlous state now,' he wrote, 'but trust me, they won't be that way for long.' He begged for patience, asking those who controlled the Church purse strings to continue to financially support his community. Why close down the poor house, he wrote, just when it was about to be transformed into a palace? In bed that night, he imagined Cabo Pasado one hundred years in the future. He saw buildings several storeys high, every last one earthquake-proof. He saw numbers falling from the heavens, and he imagined museums, and statues the size of houses, and roads with new names. He slept soundly, bouncing out of bed the following morning before sunrise, still full of batteries, ready to do God's bidding.

In response to Father Ramiro's appeal, numbers outside the Moya family home increased to twenty overnight, including several young children from the village who came with their parents and might have imagined, in the midst of the excitement, that they had stumbled on an out-of-season Independencia[15] celebration, more commonly celebrated in Chile than Carnaval.[16] Then the numbers increased to thirty. Then fifty. By now it was close to Christmas time, as carefully constructed, intricate nativity scenes in the homes of Cabo Pasado residents showed. But half those homes were now empty, their inhabitants wrapped in shawls outside the Moya residence at all hours, dancing, holding torches, saying prayers, many voices singing songs in unison like one strong voice in the darkness while their front and back doors swung open for all to see. Three days before Christmas, Alejandra shut the blinds and clicked her tongue. 'If you are a thief in Cabo Pasado in 1970,' she said, 'you can make a lifetime's profit in a week.' Ruben kept his eyes on the day's bounty, who were looking back at him, dead eyed. 'Well then,' he said to the fish, 'maybe it's time to give up the high seas.'

*

No politician can stop time. As night surely follows day 1970 was sure to be replaced by 1971, and in Santiago President Salvador Allende introduced a string of sweeping changes in education, food and housing. These rolled out all over Chile in the coming year. Blue collar workers benefited from a 35% rise in minimum wages, an astonishing jump, though Allende's detractors would no doubt point out that under his stewardship inflation stood at 22%, putting that first figure into context. A government program to tackle illiteracy came to Cabo Pasado, teaching old Rafael how to read for the first time in his eighties, and there

---

15 Independencia, or Independence Day, is the 18th of September, though celebrations in many places go on for much of the week in which the 18th falls. In modern Chile this is in stark contrast to the solemn, commemorative events connected with the anniversary of Pinochet's coup, which takes place the week before.

16 This is the week-long party which takes place all over Latin America, traditionally the last hurrah before the start of Lent. Though less prominent in Chile, where 'Independencia' (see note 26), is more fervently celebrated, this community-led celebration involving singing, the playing of instruments, marching and eating and drinking in the streets would still have been as clear in the minds of young Chileno children as Christmas is to British ones.

were other social programs too in the surrounding rural towns. But even in the days of his strongest support Allende himself admitted it was a mixed picture. The economic depression which had been growing since 1967 continued apace. The black market in foodstuffs grew and grew. The coalition which put Allende in La Moneda was splintering. All these were very public difficulties. Still, other more private things were happening too, in Allende's Chile, things not even the most powerful politician could influence, no matter how many laws were passed or proposed. For one, Alejandra Moya began to shut the blinds at Casa Moya during the day as well as the nighttime. For another, Arturo Rodgriguez reported unrest to his superiors in La Serena. And some of the older villagers said that if you listened to the mountains, listened very closely, you could hear the weather changing.

The Whole Big Thing
Extract from the memoir Writing on the Road

Sue Reid Sexton

'*The universe is made of stories, not atoms.*'
– Muriel Rukeyser, American poet and activist.

One dark night in the west of Scotland, I set off across the Cowal Peninsula all by myself in a very small campervan. The kind of super-dark darkness I found there is something I don't get in my own back garden in central Glasgow, or indeed in the outskirts where I was brought up or in any other city in which I've lived. It's a strangely mummifying darkness which that night also came with a resounding silence, something else I never get in my own patch.

If I hadn't left home at nine pm that evening, which theoretically was better late than never, I wouldn't have experienced it at all. As it was I wasn't drowned in this darkness until I'd crossed the great water of the Clyde Estuary from Gourock to Hunter's Quay near Dunoon, driven four miles north and then west, and the last of the neon streetlights had dwindled far behind me.

At the turn-off for inner deeper Cowal, which is easily missed even on a clear day in daylight, I'm reminded that the phone signal fades and dies as you head towards Portavadie. I am hoping not to meet my maker on this occasion but to find instead a quiet spot to spend the night.

The phone whistles a few space-cadet style notes then dies. I turn the van round and retrace the few hundred yards to the junction and connection, and return the call. I am on my own in a tiny van, should any of the various beasts in my mind come to life: wolves, snakes, yetis, spirits, madmen and rapists, so I am grateful that someone knows exactly where I am, what time I will have been there and where heading. My friend and I joke about the ghosts of long lost warriors of the peat bog peeking through my curtains as I undress; she reminds me that cinemas, traffic and jobs will all be waiting for me when I come back and that, in the event of panic, I can take the long drive home via the mountains at two am. Panic schmanic, I tell her. We say our goodbyes and I turn once more away from electric lamps and traffic and head again into the dark.

Like a thick blanket the forest wraps itself around me. I am in no hurry. I can stop when I like, but it's late and I'm tired. This is the first trip in a while and although I know the road I don't know how well the van will function. Stopping sooner seems better than later. My mind travels ahead. There are no cars coming to meet me, no beams slicing the night but my own. I pick a spot I haven't tried before, relax into the short drive and look forward to the melting of my everyday tensions.

There is a reservoir, held back by the appropriately named Tarsan Dam, providing storage and flow regulation for Striven hydroelectric power station. A small car park allows hydro workers to pull off and affords the public a viewing area from which to gaze down the sweep of the dam and also out across the surface of the loch. But in the pitch dark all I can see is the gravel in my headlights, the safety barrier looming out at me, the grassy verge, and a curving comma-like puddle. With no bench visible in the back of the van as a gauge, I can't tell how flat I am, so I shift about until I feel like I can't be bothered any more, then turn off the engine and the lights.

It is like being muffled by soft velvety black fur; there is no sound whatsoever. Stupidly I have no torch in the front cab so I wait in vain for my eyes to become at least a little accustomed to the super-dark dark, then gather my bag and phone. The cab light doesn't work, so this isn't easy and I don't want to do it twice. I open the door and step out, noting a slop-sound of puddle. My heart is thumping. The darkness is now heavy, weighing in on me, making my breath labour. I close the door and the noise rings out, alerting every living creature for miles that isn't already awakened to my existence. I sense heads turning, eyes piercing the night.

I watch for the ground I can't see, and fumble along the side of the van to the back door, poke the tiny key at the lock and pray I don't drop it. But it's ok. It's in and it turns and I open the door and hurry inside, and as I turn to close myself safely in I see a wedge of sky, soft with stars, still as death, ice-white above me, in the angle of the door. I am so electrified by this brief vision of heaven I shut the door and plump down wheezy on the bench inside. There is no immediate way of making sense of this panic I feel, so I look through the windows for the dark outline of bushes or hills and assume I'm scared of maniacs lurking. I close the curtains against them as quickly as I'm able.

I am in fact utterly terrified. Have I, as feared, just met my maker? I have no wherewithal whatsoever to even pinch myself and check it hurts. I am vaguely aware of this panic not being attached to any concrete source, not even maniacs in bushes. In reality, whatever that is, there is absolutely nothing to fear; I know this. I know I am probably in the safest place in the whole world but, just in case, I quickly pin the curtains tighter with bulldog clips to keep whatever monster morphs into being from engulfing me. I light my little battery lamp so I can examine the evidence, then quickly turn it off again in case I need my eyes to stay adjusted to the dark. Moreover, I wonder whether it is an act of blasphemy, punishable by who-knows-what, to disturb the darkness. And I don't want to draw attention. Wolves, I was told in countless children's stories, are attracted by light.

I try to be sensible. There is no-one out there and what exactly are these things I should be scared of anyway? I pull them out one by one and examine them, ticking them off the list of concrete reasons to be vigilant or which might justify risking the journey from the back door of the van to front cab in order to move elsewhere, somewhere lacking this unfathomable danger. Those wolves: there are none in Scotland, only talk of reintroducing them, which hasn't happened yet, as far as I know, or has it? Yetis don't exist, or do they? Not in Cowal anyway. Snakes aren't that interested in campervans because, despite my accidentally cycling over a viper in France, I know they're only deadly when provoked. Even madmen and rapists are more likely to look for prey in streets with half decent light.

Finally I have to admit it: I am scared of the sky.

Ridiculous. I laugh out loud, the act of a mad woman.

I'm reminded of chief Vitalstatistix in the Asterix stories who is afraid the sky will fall on his head. A likeable buffoon with a historically semi-accurate origin to his fear, he is the mouth-piece for Gaulish chiefs who were asked by Alexander the Great for their greatest fear. Of course! Not so daft after all. I am in good company.

Except I'm not afraid of the sky falling, I don't think. That's not it. So what exactly am I afraid of?

I hear a car approaching in the distance and am surprised that, instead of fearing abduction, I am comforted by this banal sound, the ordinary world infiltrating my overactive imagination. The car's headlights worm through the remaining gaps in the curtains, stroking the walls and table but halt against a pile of blankets. Why have they stopped? A second slice of light moves round and I realise there are two cars on the single track road. One has stopped to let the other through. I breathe a sigh of relief. Their combined light allows me a glimpse of table and bench, cooker, sink, plastic shopping bags and books lined up above the windows: normal van life, the reason I am here. I keep still, not wanting to attract any human attention. After all they could be the madmen or rapists, so I feign sleep (don't rock the van) and wait until they are gone.

In their sudden absence, the darkness is complete once more and I decide there will be no more cars on that lonely road for the rest of the night. As it happens, I'm wrong. Just as I've dared to reopen the back door, a distant flicker of light in the silence tells me there are more. I close it and wait with eyes shut for it to pass.

Then I bravely stand, give myself a shake and re-open the door a crack.

The whole icy sky gazes back at me through an inch-wide gap. I have to close the door, breathe, and argue with myself before I can open it again. I allow myself to stay inside, to keep hold of the handle and open it a little and a little more, checking the dark shapes of the bushes for wolves I know are not there, until the doorway is fully wide and I can fill it with myself and square up to the world.

The Milky Way is wispy candy floss above my head, bluey-white and stretching out across the world, a glistening cloud, and I see how it is a mass of lights and at its centre there is no space between the lights, only more light of different textures.

I move only my eyes to begin with, and without hurry, then my head, nothing more, in case I disturb anything, attract attention, bring its might crashing down on me, wake God from his slumber or disturb the entire universe. It seems best to be cautious. I decide to wait until I've stemmed this ridiculous fear, and to hold myself there for as long as it takes.

Sure enough, time passes and I am neither devoured nor vaporised. Neither do I go mad and tear my hair out or see visions. I look for constellations I can recognise, Ursulas Major and Minor, the North Star, Orion and his belt. The longer I look, the more can be seen, shimmering glittering light the nature of which and whose distance from that spot cannot even be imagined. Nothing of this sort can be truly imagined.

But heightened feelings of this kind can't be sustained for ever, as the old Buddhist idea of impermanence asserts, and my heart rate slows enough for me to realise I'm cold from standing still, and tired. I have no-one to share my awe with so it's time for bed. But as I turn inside I see this same Milky Way and the vast firmament with which I have so recently reached a quiet truce stretching in all the other directions too. Obvious, really. But I'm terrified all over again and rush back to the safety of a bench behind a closed door.

This is all, of course, completely illogical. But I am entirely helpless and this is the closest I've ever been to the God I don't believe in. I am lost. I stare at the curtains for twenty minutes debating whether I'll ever make peace between the firmament and myself, then get into my sleeping bag with a hot water bottle and weave an invisible safety bubble around me, keeping incomprehensible notions emphatically beyond the curtains. I flick through my impenetrable book about the local history of a place I've never been to, until the battery in my windup lamp makes even this impossible and I close my eyes and sleep with starlight on the brain.

Dweezils Ripped My Flesh

Tim Turnbull

Martha knows all about the avant-garde. She's one of it – of that you can be certain – whereas I, I understand nothing. It's a favourite subject anyway, but today, given the other matters which require explication, it has a special piquancy, and she is in full spate.

The dweezil, oblivious to the racket she's making, ambles, with its rolling hamster-ish gait, across its cage, takes a drink from the ceramic bowl, then flutters its little wings. It sits up, adjusts the balls of chewed up raw meat in its cheek pouches, and commences grooming. I lean against the bench, resting my chin on folded arms, and study it more carefully.

There are three types of avant-gardist, she asserts, in her well-rehearsed but slightly weary declamatory style:

a) The visionary.

This visionary is foundational. They are seers whose gift it is – and she uses gift in the sense of an endowment to the largely unappreciative populous, as well as a providentially bestowed talent – to imagine the future for us. Visionaries include William Blake and Wasilly Kandinsky. I know this already. Zappa also was one. She picks up pots and boxs then slams them down again. Whatever it is that she's looking for isn't revealing itself at the moment.

I am, as I should have known, missing the point by a fucking time zone, when I enquire in what way these luminaries showed us the actual future. They are able to see the world differently, are able to burn through the phenomenal, empiricist, bullshit, quotidian horse-shit, and really see. She emphasises the importance of this, and the depth of my ignorance, by slapping her own forehead with the tips of her fingers as if to indicate her own third eye.

I am assuming that existence unfolds along a fixed and linear path, which is why I'll never amount anything as an artist. Silly me. I'm a mere mechanic. I hardly know why she tolerates my presence.

Actually, that's not true: I do know. The reason she tolerates me and Franco – or any of the other hangers-on or assistants she's ever hired and fired – is that she's too lazy to make her own coffee, she needs an audience, and, the fact is, she likes to have pets around the place: hence also the dweezil. That's the best explanation I can come up with, anyway, for the why of the dweezil. We know it was named for the visionary previously mentioned; not after him, but, as a sort of tribute; it's named after his naming. There's a particular sort of genius associated with the naming of things. Frank had it, of course, and so does she, which is why she changed her surname to Svejniaard. It's witty, shows her common touch – a capacity for self-deprecation found only among exceptional sorts – and means that's she's not trading on her father's august cognomen.

So, the dweezil: I'm sure we'll eventually get on to the how of it, but I'm not confident I'll understand. It waddles past the eviscerated pigeon carcass to its little box of bedding. I'm fascinated by it, but resist the temptation to put my fingers near the bars. We've been there once, and I was startled at just how swift and how vicious it is.

Presently though, despite a lengthy exegesis, we are failing to arrive at an adequate explanation.

b) The proselytiser.

Why we have to go through this again, given how often I've heard it, is a mystery. No, actually the mystery is why she affects the tone of world-weariness in the telling. She clearly enjoys it. Ayn Rand and Karl Marx fall into this category. They're not blessed quite with the insight of the visionaries, but they're able to communicate what half-insights they have garnered more effectively, and thereby inspire the... not the masses exactly, but the ones who are sufficiently above the masses to appreciate the importance of the message and who provide a buttress and support for the fourth and final category, which she will be getting to.

Franco is rolling his eyes and making coffee. He's her latest and longest-serving major-domo. He minces nicely when she's about but I've seen him when she isn't, when his shoulders collapse and he carries himself like a teamster. All his light-footedness is an act. He must have a plan. Nobody would put up with this if they didn't. He's very good anyway, and found antiseptic and sticking plasters for my fingers in no time.

Me, for my part, I'm curious. Yes, there are contacts to be had, and I've sold a few pieces to clients I've met at her parties, or while accompanying her on one of her trips. I like the travel. She's generous like that. On a whim she'll say, let's go to X; the Franco of the moment will get on the phone, and off we'll go. Like the time we went down onto the streets to the Occupy Wall Street camp and it wasn't radical enough for her, or it was radical in the wrong way; so the Franco du jour was instructed and despatched, and we flew off to Paris because it was a more rigorous, or a more chic, or more theoretically interesting kind of Occupy. Kanye's visit to OWS seemed curtail interest in the movement though and she was back hard at work in the studio. She needed to be active.

c) The doer

There are people who don't have intuitive powers of the visionary, or the eloquence of the proselytiser, but they have a crude practicality and they are the doers. I've had enough of this by now, and decide to short circuit the whole oration by venturing an example:

'Like Steve Jobs, you mean?' I say. Franco, way over the other side of the studio, mimes ducking for shelter as though an air raid has just commenced. Eventually, he brings me a coffee and checks my fingers have stopped bleeding while we listen to her expound at length on that gentleman's shortcomings.

Finally, we come to the last category: the true artist; of which, it will come as no surprise to learn, she is one.

d) The true artist

They synthesise vision, expression and action, and through their fearlessness, forge new ways of seeing and being. Hence, again, the dweezil. Her old friends from Harvard and MIT may be able to gene-splice and bioengineer and posit the theoretical and technological solutions to scientific problems, but it takes real courage and originality to create solutions where there is no problem; to work entirely speculatively, unhampered by ethical, political, or imaginative constraints.

I press her to identify her collaborators, to tell me where they could have hatched this thing, but she's having none of it. It's something to do with that barn in Wyoming where she keeps the components of her bigger installations, I'm fairly sure of that. That's why I haven't seen so much of her for the past six months. I have a pretty good idea who she's working with; it's that Julius Kelp-a-like Morry or whatever he calls himself. She's not nearly as smart as she thinks.

I wonder what I'd have been able to do with her cash and start in life; then there's an excruciating pain in my arm and I jerk away dragging the dweezil cage with me. While musing, I've leant against it and the fucking animal has chewed through my jacket sleeve and sunk its vicious little fangs into the soft flesh of my upper arm. Franco grabs the cage but it won't let go till it's torn a chunk out of me.

'You're going to have to get rid of that thing,' I say. 'Kill it. It's dangerous.'

Franco attempts to patch me up. It hurts like hell, and my shirt and second best jacket are ruined. I'm tempted to take the hammer from her workbench and batter the horrid little thing to a paste.

*

The row was so intense that I don't see her for months. She doesn't answer emails; her phone's perpetually routed to voicemail, which leads me to suspect that I'm being blocked. After a while I give up, reasoning that I'm getting more of my own work done because I'm spending less time acting as a sounding board for her. When the call comes it catches me completely by surprise. I compose myself before I answer, take a deep breath, and exhale as I press the button so that I'm smiling as I speak.

'Martha, how lovely...' but I'm pulled up short.

'Benjamin. You've got to get down here. It's escaped. I've locked it in the studio. Oh God. Help.'

I try to calm her, but she's listening even less than usual, and making far less sense.

'The what?' I ask.

'The manticore. It got loose.' I think I've misheard at first, but after further grilling I establish that what I think I heard really is what she said. She adds that Franco may be injured. I say I'm on my way; give me thirty or forty minutes. She asks me if I have a gun. I don't, of course, and I suggest if she thinks I need one then it might be time to get the police involved. After a few more minutes of histrionics, I hang up and set off.

It takes me thirty five minutes to get there, during which time I have to field another couple of calls, neither of which are any more coherent than the first. She's sitting in the lobby. There's a broom shaft through the handles of the studio entrance's double fire door. She has a hand gun and a box of ammunition. There are bullets rolling around on the floor.

'Load this,' she says, thrusting the pistol and its magazine at me.

'What is going on, Martha?' I ask, ignoring her entreaty.

The manticore has gotten loose. Franco was trying to clean it out and it got by him.

Ignoring the obvious question – what in the name of Jesus is the manticore – I ask where Franco is. She indicates the other side of the door.

'And the... err?'

'Manticore. You've got to kill it.'

I take the pistol from her, raise myself from the squatting position, and peer through the safety glass of the studio door. There's no sign of anyone, or anything. The benches are covered, as usual, with sketches, spray cans, tools, paints and brushes. The big machine at the far end, which she'd been using to fire randomised patterns of pigment at huge canvasses hung on the wall, doesn't look as though it's seen any action since I was last here. The kitchenette in the corner, Franco's domain, is the tidiest part of the room as usual.

A movement between the workbenches attracts my attention. A dog's head has hove into view from behind one of the sturdy wooden tables. It looks like a German Shepherd, but an especially unhealthy specimen with weepy eyes. It's nodding as though palsied.

'What's that dog doing in there?' I ask.

She's on her feet in a flash.

'That's it,' she says. 'That's the manticore.'

'It's a dog.' I say, but even as the words are leaving my mouth, it lurches forward, and I see it isn't just a dog. It has the front legs, head and shoulders of a German Shepherd but one whose fur is patchy; it appears at first sight to have some sort of skin condition. As it moves, it seems convulsed, and this is explained when its whole body is revealed. From halfway down its trunk the coat gives way to chitinous shell, and where there should be a hind leg are three segmented arthropod legs. They cycle in the air, sometimes touching the ground, sometimes not. Its rear end tapers into a proper but massive scorpion tail. It moves as if on an eccentric cam, lurching and limping, and I can see that this is because on its other flank the arthropod legs are mixed with a deformed canine leg.

I'm stunned.

'What in God's name possessed you?' I say.

''You've got to kill it,' she says. 'Franco's still in there. I think he may be hurt.'

'May be hurt, Martha?' I can't even bring myself to continue this conversation. I pick up the magazine from the floor and start to stuff it with bullets.

'It may have stung him,' she says. 'You know how to shoot. That's why I had to call you.'

I slam the magazine home and tell her to shut up, then I remove the broom from the door handles.

'I'm going to find Franco. I want you to call the police and an ambulance. I don't want to hear. Just do it.'

The thing has moved off between the furniture and I've lost sight of it. I slip through the door, moving very slowly, with the gun in both hands. I don't take a step until I've checked all around me, and in this way I make my way towards where I last saw it. The room has a strange echoey acoustic when it isn't being filled by Martha. I call Franco's name softly but there's no reply. From over the next bench comes a scrabbling, scratching sound.

I get as far back from the sound as possible and crane around the corner. The thing is turning awkwardly in the passage between bench and storage shelves. It appears to be distressed by simply moving, panting and mouthing at the air. When it sees me it bares its teeth and lets out a strangled parody of a bark. At the same time the scorpion tail rears up and flicks at the air. It begins to move toward me.

I raise the gun, take very careful aim, and loose off a shot. The thing bows under the impact and emits another fearful noise. The shot rings in my ears and from behind me I think I hear a whirring sound. I glance over my shoulder quickly but see nothing there. The thing's been hit and there is a wound in its torso, but it still scrabbles toward me. I fire again. It echoes round the room and I hear the whirring, like someone flicking through a pack of cards. The thing is still moving. I fire shot after shot until the magazine is empty and the monstrosity lies lifeless in a pool of ichorous discharge. I find a length of wood on a workbench and prod it. The tail stirs in what I take to be a reflex, but it's quite dead.

'Franco,' I call, but there's no answer. I skirt the thing and see over near the paint-firing machine Franco's legs poking out from behind a stack of paint cans. I shout louder but he doesn't stir. I shout back to the door to tell Martha the thing is dead and ask if she's called the ambulance. There's no answer from her either.

I'm still cautious, but reason that she used 'manticore' in the singular, and move to where Franco lies. I tell him that an ambulance is on the way, so as to reassure him, but when I step round the paint cans I fall silent. By Franco's head is a smashed crate. It looks as though he knocked it down as he fell to the floor. I can see that he too is quite dead. There's a puddle of blood around his head and movement across his body. It takes a moment to register what this is. I feel my pulse quicken. Crawling all over him, tearing holes in his flesh, are two dozen, or maybe more, little leather-winged rodent things: dweezils. I hope they'll remain fully occupied until I can get out of the room. I back away very, very slowly.

Sonnet for my Favourite Supermarket

Calum Rodger

’his poem starts with an apostrophe
LIDL you are WONDERFUL! I <3U
Your logo my constant yellow and blue
I love your tomatoes, pesto and coffee
O, your ranges! So neat and untyrannical
You agree brand selection is no genuine choice
You wear Saltire badges even though you are Deutsch
And your checkout staff so admirably mechanical!
I only visit when it’s dark and the moon is out
I prepare myself by feeding my head on violins
O, you glow so much! You are a happy large machine
Meanwhile the universe is expansive and full of doubt
You are its opposite! If only you sold skins!
I will go to you tonight and I will fill my heart with beans.

what do the gaps in poems mean?

Andrew Blair

what do the bits of poems mean when the words aren't there what is space how can nothing mean so many gaps in every piece right justified ignorance more or less than text is there some sort of coarse savant process is there some sort of course heired literary strategy what technique poetry is supposed to look like that so it does until it doesn't do you see no of course not for it is nothing that you are looking at and are there words for it so does that make it nothing when there are words where there are names there are tokens esteemed learned disciplined you must not be this taught to go on the ride on time and pace hail the glorious dead space open to one to all things must end I suppose this nothing forthcoming is distinct how would we know we cannot just assume it must be so else where does this poem end I have a theory and I will explain it below as simply as I can:

It's as simple as that.

Is this poem going to consist solely of the words 'Why is it okay for John Martyn to be a wifebeating arsehole but not Chris Brown?' because I am unable to express that sentiment in a way that embraces my fondness for ambiguity while showing off my frankly stupendous vocabulary (You're welcome)

Andrew Blair

It isn't.

Oranges Are Not the Only Fruit (Thank Fuck)

Calum Rodger

Damn you oranges y u so hard to open?
I have found myself flighty with fruit before
But I am anguishing in promises of citrus
Pathetic flakes of peel are falling to the floor
Is it even litter if it's biodegradable?
Hm, whatever, I don't care anymore
To hell with these peals of uncivil laughter
Reverberating through my every pore!
My vitamin-deficient heart is breaking
Oh give me a Satsuma, or something with a core!
Orange, you've put me through the juicer
You're dead to me – I'm going to the store
And if it's me you want to find
You will know me by the trail of the rind

Lyrical Commands

Nick-e Melville

The untold story of the Witches of Oz
distract their attention without good cause

Don't bring death to your door
 Try praying
For the moments that matter
Know more

This is your final warning
Together we can make it better

Be a Great Westerner
Baghdad calls for us to send in air strikes
volunteer today

It's in our nature
securing a better future

Be The Best
best of the best
building a greater West

It makes life Better

Persuading People
For life
This is the life
system change

Remember   antibiotics won't help your defences
The experts at the AA have created these maps

GET SET FOR NEW
let's have a proper brew
Complete with waterfall taps

If not you, Nicky, who?

it's a real worry
no man has something to do now
Tomorrow

Hurry
Hurry Ends Thursday
Learn, escape and enjoy

Respect My Privacy
immediately

We are watching you   it's nice to be looked after
we're listening   We search
The trams are coming
YO!ToGo GO ARGOS GO TALIBAN GO

there's a runner in all of us
Run and Become
          dangerous
nature is nuts
Do not chew or crush the tablets
Amazing journeys start here

Welcome to the emergency department
Smoking when pregnant harms your baby
My son told me he was okay
I eat my five portions of fruit & vegetables every day

restart your heart
LIVE IT
restart your heart
Powered by RoadPilot

Simple Enjoyment
chicken is important
I eat bread, pasta and potatoes to help me play
to help you navigate Britain's roads safely and easily

EAT REPEAT

A large glass of wine has the same calories as a doughnut
pinot grigio?
Drink with respect to yourself and your mates
see you on page thirty eight

No drinks on the dance floor
THIS. IS. LAGER.

SIT
LIKE YOU'VE EARNT IT

HORSES
We want the best of both worlds
FROM RESPONSIBLE SOURCES

the people who give you extra are coming to Edinburgh
people with cancer need places like these
Patients we want you
Rolling out across hotels
up our street
Where your shopping can become our treat

Banking that works around you   We hear you
Keep your belongings with you
No cash held on these premises overnight

The world is yours

You're Due a Deuchars
ways to make your friends and family jealous
Travel by bus: a great day out

movement is happiness
It's on us

Nobody wants their child to be lonely
See inside for details
In emergency pull to open
It is advised that children should occupy lower berths
Store in a clean dry place, away from sunlight,

Tell us ten things   this is how it works

      We recycle oils to make diesel fuel for our trucks
      No stopping except buses
      your life is your work
      Your Issues Make Our Issues
      work sucks
      Escape for lunch
      Take a break
      Grow to work
      Join our team
      Private Car Park

Tiredness can kill   lunch doesn't have to
Your customers do

THEY GAVE THEIR LIVES FOR THEIR COUNTRY AND FOR FREEDOM
Make sure to clean them

PLEASE FIX GUARD RAIL
AND STILL
Secure yourself
Life... is an adventure
The perfect centre

Relaxation is skill and comes with practise
Be prepared on your journey... just in case

model shown varies from UK spec
Don't get scared, get checked

Now's the time for superfast broadband
      better by far
unless the permission of the publisher has been given beforehand
      for you and your car

Passengers must not speak to the driver
Thank you for reading this poster

who says there's nothing good on TV?
88% of women agree

Pigeonholes

Ian Newman

i.

A step onto the stone spiral –
Rationally grey, not golden –
Through a door ajar discovered
On University grounds;

A young man abroad
In his home city, curiously
Wandering between lectures
With nothing to kill but time,

Clambers up the unlit stairway –
Unlit, but arrowslit –
Notices first a feather,
Next a splodge, leavings

Of a trapped pigeon.
Here is its skeleton now
Behind an unused office door –
Laid to rest on this cold floor.

Something profound should happen,
Some epiphany should come,
Some elegiac and affirming thought
Cries out to be had – and is not.

He emerges from this phony parapet,
This accidental mausoleum –
A monument to entropy –
Into the cold afternoon air.

ii.

Please place your response
In the pigeonhole provided.

Responsibility to provide
Is in holes, pigeon placed.

The pigeon's response hole
Is pleased with providence.

Please pigeon your holes
With the provided response.

A play doesn't exist until it's done, you don't write plays to not be done... with poems you're able to make a little thing that's finished with each poem – and that's what you're trying to do. It's something that exists. I think of it as a shape of sound in silence, but of course you've got to put that down on a page.

Liz Lochhead

The Gutter Interview:

Liz Lochhead

The Gutter
Interview:
Liz Lochhead

Liz Lochhead was born in Motherwell in 1947 and grew up in Newarthill, Lanarkshire. She studied at the Glasgow School of Art and taught at schools in Glasgow and Bristol. After graduating from GSA in 1970, she went a few times to the extra-mural writers' workshop run by Philip Hobsbaum at Glasgow University. In 1971 she won a Radio Scotland poetry competition, in 1972 she read with Norman MacCaig at a poetry festival in Edinburgh, and her first collection, *Memo for Spring*, was published and won a Scottish Arts Council Book Award. She met Alasdair Gray, Jim Kelman and Tom Leonard in this period, and later in the decade Tom McGrath and Alan Spence.

In 1978 her second collection, *Islands*, was published and she wrote and performed in *Sugar and Spite* at the Traverse, Edinburgh. She was awarded the first Scottish/Canadian Writers' Exchange Fellowship the same year, and went to Toronto, then lived in the USA after the fellowship ended. Over the next couple of years she returned to New York for lengthy periods and became a full-time writer, performance poet and broadcaster.

Her plays include *Blood and Ice* (1982), first performed at the Edinburgh Traverse in 1982; *Mary Queen of Scots Got Her Head Chopped Off* (1989), first performed by Communicado Theatre Company at the 1987 Edinburgh festival; *Dracula* (1989); *Cuba* (1997), a play for young people commissioned by the Royal National Theatre for the BT National Connections Scheme; and *Perfect Days* (1998), a romantic comedy, first performed at the Edinburgh festival in 1998. She translated and adapted Molière's *Tartuffe* (1985) into Scots, and it premiered at the Edinburgh Royal Lyceum in 1987. The script of her adaptation of Euripides' *Medea* (2000) for Theatre Babel won the Saltire Society Scottish Book of the Year Award. And in 2002 she wrote *Misery Guts*, based on Molière's *The Misanthrope*, in which the action is updated to the Scottish Parliament. Her work for television includes *Latin for a Dark Room*, a short film, screened as part of the BBC Tartan Shorts season at the 1994 Edinburgh International Film Festival, and *The Story of Frankenstein* for Yorkshire Television. In just the last few years her latest works 'Edwin Morgan's Dreams and Other Nightmare's' and 'Mortal Memories' have been premiered and seen second runs.

She has received honorary degrees from, it seems, most universities in Scotland. Her sixth collection of poetry, *The Colour of Black and White*: Poems 1984-2003, was published in 2003 and two years later she succeeded Edwin Morgan as Poet Laureate of Glasgow following his own appointment as Scots Makar – in which post she followed Morgan's after his death in 2011. Her most recent book is *A Choosing: The Selected Poetry of Liz Lochhead* (2011) and she is working on a further collection to mark her five years as Makar.

Gutter: You come from an art school background, how important to you, when you are writing poetry is the look of the poem on the page? Reading back over some of your earlier work like *Memo for Spring*, there is a visual element there: you experimented a bit with different layouts, variable margins,

LL: Yeah you always do a wee bit of that with poetry. The layout of a poem is as much to make it readable, as to make it hearable, actually. That's what I'm usually doing; I'm trying to do something that will make people hear it as they read it. Voice is the thing that is the most important to me in poetry, though. I don't do much experimentation of the concrete kind. But I really enjoy Edwin Morgan's, you know, looking at them and sort of loving the fun that he got out of them and, you know, James MacGonagil, who I think of as very much in that tradition. He's Eddy's wonderful biographer, but he's a very, very fine poet in his own right. It's not the experimental side of Eddy that's the closest to me and my own practice, which is always about sound and voice and sometimes rhymes and rhythm. Layout on the page and certainly illustration doesn't appeal to me at *all* with poetry, really, because you try and illustrate your poem as you're doing it. The words should make the pictures. I'm interested in image, but the images that are contained in the words if heard out loud.

Although, when I've been drawing recently – and I've been drawing a lot over the past ten years – I've been putting words on the drawings a lot.

Gutter: Almost like found text?

LL: Yeah, or make that part of the image of the drawing. But it's different. That's words as part of the images of a drawing. I wouldn't make drawings part of a poem. It's a different thing. Although I've got nothing against, you know – when you make a book, and you want the book to look nice and you want to pick the right font and of course you play around with line endings and shapes and so on, of course you do. Because it's part of what'll help – there's got to be something that – and it's a different thing with every *poem* – but there's got to be something that makes it a poem rather than a bit of prose.

It's the sort of raising-up of the voice and that might be a formalising of rhythms that are in it or, there'll be something that makes it... a poem. And then there're also other things I think of as songs, or entertainments. And I don't know why I call them songs, but you know, they're kind of a step-down from a poem. It's silly; it's just all in my own head.

Gutter: No, that's an interesting way to make a distinction.

LL: I mean, you've got wee things that you do that are your own. Because, the thing about writing poems is: you're doing it for yourself, you know. A poem exists, even if it's lying around under the bed not typed up. A play doesn't exist until it's done, you don't write plays to not be done...

Gutter: They only exist when they're performed.

LL: Whereas, with poems you're able to make a little thing that's finished with each poem – and that's what you're trying to do. It's something that exists. I think of it as a shape of sound in silence, but of course you've got to put that down on a page. And I do like to read poems on the page.

Gutter: That's what I was going to ask you, because obviously I think of you very much as a performer of your work and I think many other people would too, but do you enjoy experiencing poems as text on a page as much as you do speaking them aloud?

LL: Oh, yes, you must! But that text on the page is an attempt to write down *voice*. You do need to see it on the page as well, because, you know, I'm not that interested in writing things that will give up all their mysteries on a single hearing. Although some things do – a song, maybe. Some songs, maybe you'd only have to hear them once to get anything out of them that's in them and of course you don't know if there's anything in them for anybody else except yourself, anyway. But they cannae lock you up for it.

Gutter: you're a poet with a very distinctive voice and voice is, as you said, at the heart of what you do, but you also came from this visual arts background. Just how important is image to you in creating a poem?

LL: I think at first, particularly, I was trying to put down pictures of things in words. The poems that I was interested in reading when I was at art school were like that – one of the things that delighted me was the way that McCaig would say something in words and you would just hear it, you know, and you would just *see it*, you know?

Like when he would describe a toad and say "Stop looking like a purse." and, I would get this image of a purse, it would be funny. And so it's the image of how things look – the things you are writing about, I mean – not the piece of writing not the image of it on a page. It's a record, it's a score. And I do work on that bit of it. You know, the point when you start to type it up into the computer. I wouldn't be able to write it first on a computer, you'd need lots of drafts, but once you begin to muck about with it, see it...

Gutter: That's interesting. Tom Leonard told me that he drafts very much on the computer because he likes the ability to play with...

LL: From the start?

Gutter: From the start with how he sets the text on the page.

LL: Absolutely. Yeah, Tom is absolutely one of these people who are putting down voices on a page. But the shape of it, the look – are so vital that it's about half of what he's doing. He has been like that right from the start, I mean these wonderful punning ways of spelling Glaswegian for instance in *Six Glasgow Poems*, you know. Where it would say "Ma right insane yirra pape.", you know, would be a spelling of "'M I right", then "in sayin'". It was interesting, I felt that at first, one of the things that Tom was doing was writing down exact Glaswegian sounds but as if for an RP speaker to speak it. It was very funny, things like "Ma right insane yirra pape" – that would be a way of getting an Oxbridge Professor to say it correctly like a Glaswegian.

I mean, Tom's a jeweller and a

precisionist, but I'm not. I'm quite splashy and messy. I've got a sort of beat element to me. Although I try and get them as short as I can, but I'm not a six line poet, you know. A sonnet is about as wee as I can get.

Gutter: Is that the painter talking? You were an art teacher for a long time and you said you are still drawing

LL: It's a different thing, a different thing. What I mostly like about drawing is *not* being wordy about it. I find it difficult to write about art and that's why I feel sorry for a lot of people that are at the Art School these days, because they're asked to write beforehand, what they want to do before they do it, which is just stupid.

I mean, the way I know that most artists work – and I'm talking about every medium – and of course by the time you're sixty-seven, like I am, you know a lot of people who work in very different ways and, you know, in the world of music, in the world of painting – abstract or figurative – or writing, or even writing plays: how most people that I've met seem to go about it is they're following a small hunch and not knowing if it'll get anywhere. They wouldn't be able to write in advance what they're going to write about or paint about. They just know they want to do *this* and see where it leads. And that's actually the way art – of *all* sorts – by-and-large happens. And yet, nowadays, people are asked, if you're doing a creative writing degree, to write a PhD about your practice while you're doing it. It just seems to me as if something that could not fail to be really bad for you.

I mean, I met a young painter recently – a wonderful and very successful young painter. He was saying that at art college, which he only left about four or five years ago, he used to mock up all the pre-work *after* he had done the paintings. He would write his method and his ambitions and his reasons for it *afterwards*. You know, mock it up because he had to write something. Total nonsense. I'm angry at the moment, because I think we should be able to call out the people who are teaching false wisdom.

We should be able to say to them: "No, I'm not actually going to do that. I'll maybe write about it afterwards, if you want me to, but I'm not going to pretend that I planned all this before, because that's not how it happens." It's perpetuating a lie and we're allowing them to perpetuate a lie, the teachers and the people who come into art schools, creative writing departments, this and that, and they try to set up a false academic framework round what is instinctual, exploratory and, in the end, mysterious.

Gutter: Do you think that's responsible for the decline of the avant-garde, or of risk-taking in literature? Particularly if you look at Scotland at the moment, there are a lot of very exciting visual artists around, but in terms of my generation and younger in the literary arts, there are not many people making things new. Well, maybe that's not fair...

LL: I suppose, with either of my artistic interests, I don't necessarily look for new stuff to be what I'm reading. New to me! But that might be a bit of Henryson. That's what I bought recently, you know, a wee book – I was down in Moffat and in a book shop and there was a little slim volume: *MacDiarmid's selection of Henryson* and I thought "That's great." And it's full of things that I didn't know because I haven't had a literary education. I've read a lot in my life, but I've not studied English literature, so I don't have an overview or a historical sweep attached to it, you know.

And I didn't have to have that with art. At Art School you were allowed to like Rouault and Jackson Pollock without having to put them in a certain progression through history. In my day, you could just like them as artists and take what you wanted from it. And I think that's what artists try and do, by-and-large in all mediums, music too.

Gutter: Do you think the Academy is too strong a presence? As an editor, it took me a while to get over my sense of outsiderness, because I don't have a formal literary education either. So I taught myself, had a kind of magpie approach and obviously missed a lot of things as well, which led to insecurity on my part. Is that something you've felt as well when you started?

LL: No, because I never sort of thought of myself as a writer. I always thought "Oh, I'm just- I'm writing this just now." I never thought of *myself* as a writer, I thought of *this bit of writing* that I'm doing and I see what it's like. And I've always expected not necessarily to be doing it right. I think all artists are self-taught. I'm not saying you don't teach yourself via reading, listening, looking at other stuff, but you pick out the people that have done things that you're really interested in and you do your own versions of that and

nobody ever calls you out on what it was or says you were influenced by this or that, which always has amazed me, you know. But I think you emulate aspects of other artists you like. My favourite writer in the world – my favourite living writer – is the wonderful Alice Munro. Of course she writes out of an interest in life and she's a wonderful observer of human nature. When you read her it gives you back so much of the people you have known in your own life. Just with identifying with the very precise way she captures experience – what human beings would *do*.

And then she's got great *stories*, great *events*. But she said that it's not her interest in life that made her a writer, it's her interest in writing. It's the writers that have made her want to write rather than, you know, a wee story or an observation about it. I suppose it's setting up your own experience and comparing it and contrasting it with how other writers have written about this before. And feeling that, despite the fact they've maybe done it very well, you've got the right to do it all over again. Not necessarily anew, but you've got the right to do it all over again.

Gutter: So do you think, as you've gone through life and acquired more experience, more exposure, do you think your creative process has changed?

LL: I think the best I would be able to get out of that one would be that I'd say that as you get more experienced in both life and whatever pursuit you're doing, you might – or might not! – be more accurate about the kind of hunches and pursuits that are going to lead somewhere, but that's about it.

Luckily, I'm writing again and it's working well for me – which doesn't mean that it's working well in terms of other people – and when I feel as if I'm finding out some things that I want to do, I might be wrong about the writing going well but I don't *feel* wrong about it.

So whenever I'm in that state when I'm writing, when I'm trying to find out some things, it has the same kind of excitement as it used to have. By-and-large, it never means as much to anybody else as your early work did. When you were cooking with gas, when you were early and more naïve about it

An artist friend of mine was saying to me the other week: artists don't get better as they get older, but you do have to keep doing it. And you never know, you might get on a good theme again, but he said- you know, "Only Rembrandt got better as he got older". And he said, "But right enough, early Rembrandt's pretty good!"

Gutter: So how do you feel now, looking back at your early poems, like *Memo for Spring*?

LL: I don't.

Gutter: You don't? You must have looked back at them when you put your *Selected* together...

LL: "A Choosing". Which was a nod to one of the poems that I knew would go in: 'The Choosing'. I don't think it's that great as a poem, but it means a lot to people, more than a lot of things that I've written later that I might think are better. But, you know, you can't argue with what meant something to people. I suppose what I feel

like when I look at something like "The Choosing" – I feel like that was written by somebody else, that used to be me, you know? So, I don't dislike it, but I don't feel a desire to write like that again.

I feel a desire to keep writing with that kind of enjoyment and luckily, at the moment, I'm at a period like that. I've been really enjoying the things I've been writing over the last four or five years. Not that I've been enormously prolific, but more prolific in poetry anyway than I've been for a few years. So, yeah, I do feel as if I'm onto a time when I'm enjoying doing it and it'll be for other people to judge whether they're any good or not, it'll be for other people to judge whether or not they're very different from what I used to do or if they're very much the same. I don't know. I just – you always think you're doing something very different and then when you look back twenty years later you don't think you were. But you always feel, you've always got to be feeling you're trying to find out something new: technically or whatever. I don't mean anything new and startling, not that other people haven't done before, but things that *you* haven't done before.

Gutter: One of the attractive things about your work is the twin strands of your poetry and your drama. How do you think in thirty years' time people will mainly remember you: a dramatist or a poet?

LL: I don't know.

Gutter: You don't know?

LL: I don't know. If at all! I mean, who knows? There are all kinds of people that were, well not so much in literature... but there are all kinds of, say, painters that were a big deal in the thirties and forties that nobody looks at now. I'm not worried about that. God almighty, I don't feel posterity calling. No, I'm just trying to enjoy writing things and so far in life, not always, but by-and-large I've been lucky in that if I'm truthful about what I'm really interested in, I've tended to interest some other people, you know.

Sometimes less people than a previous strand I was on, but usually, if I'm being honest about what I really find interesting and really want to write about, it's so far tended to appeal to some of the people that are interested in poetry, somebody at a bus stop said to me: "Are you famous?" [scoffs] "No!" And they said, "Somebody there told me you were famous." And I said: "Name a famous poet." And he said, "Er... Robert Burns." And I said "Well then." No, I write poetry, but I'm certainly not famous. But, you know, I suppose in the world of poetry in Scotland, people would've heard of one and usually dislike intensely what one does or whatever, you know what I mean?

Gutter: You're well kent.

LL: You know, I don't care. It doesnae matter. No. No. I'm not worried about historical whatevers or fitting into a sequence, and I wasn't aware of being a female role model, for instance. That's what people are often grateful to me for: for blazing a track for womankind. I was just blazing a track for me, you know? And I didn't really think of myself as a woman writer, at first. It never occurred to me that I didn't have the right to write because I was a woman. I suppose I noticed that there was a bit of a shortage of them in Scotland, I

mean I'm not that thick, you know, but I still didn't think that meant that one wouldn't be listened to or heard.

In fact, it was jolly useful at first. I wouldn't have been the only woman writing in Scotland, writing poetry in Scotland, of course, I would be far from it – but I was the only one that was getting published or noticed at that time. So I got to be the one woman on very a many a four poet panel. You know, they would think, "We'd better have a woman." So there'd be any three out of about twelve old guys – they're mostly dead now –but I'd be number four because they knew I would do it. So I was the token woman. That was alright.

Gutter: So there'd be MacCaig and Garioch and MacLean and...

LL: Yeah. Me! Or... Josh Bruce... maybe Scott... Edwin Morgan and me! Or whatever. So, I was jolly lucky, you know. I've been a very lucky person in my life.

Gutter: In previous interviews you've said that you've never regarded yourself as a trailblazer, but that you are grateful that people have regarded you in that way.

LL: Oh absolutely. Well, when somebody like Ali Smith says that, you know, finding my poems really, really changed their life. But you know, I would have been the same with Denise Levertov or something. I would have been thrilled to find her. I wouldn't have been able to think "But she lives in Glasgow". That would be an extra and it was an extra for Ali, you know. She could be a woman, a writer and she can live in Scotland.

of course, there had been precedents, you know, but there weren't really many.

Helen Cruikshank was in her eighties. She was published just before me by the same publisher and MacDiarmid had said of her: "Helen has the gift o' sang." Which was a kind of put-down, I felt. He was being kind of patronising. "The gift o' sang..." Because there was a sexist culture in society in general, literary society was not free of it. But I didn't suffer from it myself. I was very, very lucky, I was allowed to do it and not be a muse. I'm very proud to say I've never slept with a poet. Which is not true.

Gutter: Do you want me to stop the tape?

LL: No, no, it's fine. I had a lovely lover in Canada: but that's the only person I've ever been close to in that way that was a poet, or thought of himself as a poet. You know, I've been lucky enough to be a great chum of many male poets in my life and, you know, my contemporaries and friends. I'm one of the guys as far as they're concerned, I'm glad to say. And always have been!

Gutter: You were in that fortunate position of being in the vanguard of quite an exceptional bunch of women writers: there was Carol Ann Duffy, Jackie Kay and more widely there's Margaret Atwood, Eavan Boland, Sharon Olds, Alice Notley, all from that similar generation.

LL: I mean, Atwood in Canada, she had just blazed a complete trail. I came across Atwood, just when I was about thirty because she wasn't – at that time she wasn't getting here, you know. When I went to Canada, it was a bit like Scottish culture – it existed in its own bubble. This is more than thirty years ago, now. It was nineteen... It's nearly forty years ago, now.

Canadian writing was stuck in a way that American fiction wasn't. So there were great North American writers like Margaret Lawrence, Alice Munro and Atwood and they were only famous in Canada. It was just beginning to change, but I'm sure that I'm one of the first people in Britain to have read Alice Munro. Her work came out here very shortly after I came back from Canada. And, you know, I mean I meet people frequently who just love short story writing and say Alice Munro's just the master. She's as good as Chekov; she's a great short story writer. But, also around that time I was living in a country with a great short story writer called Jim Kelman, who's a major writer, especially of short fiction, I think.

Gutter: Oh, it's brilliant, yeah.

LL: I mean I like the novels very, very much, but it's Jim Kelman's short fiction that blows me away. You know, something like a story of him going to the doctor, I could read it and re-read it and think: "This is as good as Kafka in its own way." And sometime he will get out there and be regarded widely across the world in a way that... I mean he is regarded widely in Britain and America and by people that *know*. But, there hasn't been that international break-through, especially not in Britain. But in Canada when I went there Canada was under the cultural imperialism of America.

And just as we, in this country are under London. I mean it's breaking through. I mean, Ali Smith's just won the Orange Prize. I must –I must text her and go "Oh Ali that's great and for such a great book!" But the Scottish women writers that did break through – more widely than I've ever broken through – they're slightly younger than me that's great, you know! Kathleen Jamie, she's a good ten years younger than me.

Gutter: Alison Kennedy and Janice Galloway...

LL: Yeah, they're all ever so slightly younger. You know, I mean, not much... But the same thing was happening in Canada with regards to America. There's still quite a lot of cultural imperialism in Britain, you know, the English side of the English-speaking world. There's the Scottish *art scene*- Scottish painting – these are generalisations – or Scottish writing, or the more typically Scottish of the Scottish writers and painters have got a slightly different sensibility from the standard English sensibility. Of course, there's other people writing, usually from the North of England, or from the assumed South of England, or from marginalised areas like gay or extremely poor, or fantasy genre, there's various other kinds of people that are breaking through. But, you know, the standard English hegemony still exists and thinks it's the only one.

It doesn't bother me, but it does...

Gutter: In my research I happened upon your British council page, which describes you as, in inverted commas: "very much a Scottish writer".

LL: Well, that's good.

Gutter: I disagree with that because of your international translations in both directions.

LL: Oh no, I'm very happy to be very much a Scottish writer. Just as I'm very happy to be a woman writer, because both those things are not controversial – they're just facts.

I don't like being called a "feminist-writer", hyphen, or a "Scottish-hyphen-writer", or a writer in Scots. Because I'm not a writer in Scots – except sometimes when I want to be. But being a very Scottish writer, I don't mind having a sensibility that'll have a flavour of my country in it. You know, I think Peter Carey is an Australian writer. These are things that are just facts. And there's nothing wrong with being a Scottish writer that could pass as an English writer, either if that's just the way you wrote. But I don't think I would come across as standard English, because I am interested in non-standard and non-patrician things.

I'll read somebody like Martin Amis – his book *Experience* I think is fantastic, I've not liked his recent novels very much, but his early novels I liked, the very transgressive ones. But, in his book Experience: he'll sort of say, you know, "My father and Philip Larkin are the only poets who ever..." And I know fine he's not read any Morgan, MacCaig, whatever. He's missing them out by having ignored them!

By just never having explored it. They still think they've got the right to have this little group and a lot of very good writers are part of it. I was reading Julian Barnes writing about art recently in the Guardian and I've enjoyed a lot of Julian Barnes' stuff. I've liked his work, I've liked the things he's written about grief, I found them very interesting and comforting. But there he was, pontificating about art, from his point of view, but without any sense that his point of view was anything other than *the* point of view. That's what annoys me, that it's *the* point of view, it seemed to me he was writing about art, knowing fuck-all about art, actually. It was very literary writing about art. It was somebody that wasn't really interested in painting, but interested in literature, was writing about art. I'll look at more of it, I've only read the one in the Guardian and it did and didn't interest me. It was the bit where he says: "One grows out of so-and-so" and you think: "*You* did. Take the responsibility for the fact that this is your personal point of view, rather than speaking as if there's a point of view that's generally recognised that you are speaking from."

Gutter: It's lacking in any sort of self-regard or self-examination.

LL: Aye. Lacking in any sense of positioning yourself as being marginal because everybody's marginal. I think it's interesting to, just accept the way you're marginal and think you've got the right to speak, write, compose from that point of view. But not to think that, of course, everybody's part of the mainstream, and of course, that the word from the mainstream will be the most valuable – because it's no more valuable than any other marginal places to come from.

Gutter: Do you think that's why it's so hard for Scottish writers to be regarded as anything else than provincial by London? You know, it strikes me that Irish writing gets taken a lot more seriously by London.

LL: Well, yes, yes! This interests me. And that's a case for Scottish independence, maybe a non-political case for it. I think

Ireland is regarded as another country that speaks English but has its own culture and a literary culture that literary England could treat as an equal. They don't think that about Welsh literature, gay literature, science-fiction literature, Scottish literature. There's various ways of being marginalised, but you don't think of it as being quite the thing, you know.

Gutter: Were you not told that *Mary Queen of Scots...* was "far too Scottish for us". Was that not true?

LL: The truth of that anecdote is: I wrote *Mary Queen of Scots* twenty-eight years ago and the *National Theatre – the National Theatre* – said it.

At that time I had a lovely agent – he was murdered ten years ago, yeah, a wonderful man, I loved him, he was one of my best friends as well – he'd been educated in Scotland, he was a fantastic literary agent. So he, of course, when he took me up sent *Mary Queen of Scots* to the National Theatre, with a sort of "Oh, I see that you're going to do *Maria Stuart* – Schiller's *Maria Stuart* – in the big theatre, what about this very interesting play to put on?"

And the National Theatre, somebody in the literary department – and they shall be nameless because I don't know who they were! – said, "This is a fantastic play, but far too Scottish for us." My agent was furious with that, but I thought "Well yeah, it probably is too Scottish for them." I just accepted that. He was angry.

But my friend David Greig recommended *Mary Queen of Scots Got her Head Chopped Off* to the National Theatre of Scotland when it was set up, and well they couldn't take his advice completely, but when they did Schiller's *Maria Stuart* I remember saying jocularly: "Well I said that *Mary Queen of Scots Got her Head Chopped Off* was too Scottish for the National Theatre, but fuck's sake, I did not think it would be too Scottish for the National Theatre of Scotland!"

Gutter: So, they did say yes to it eventually?

I mean it was a while before that that the National Theatre of Scotland did it, but only in a very small touring version.

Gutter: I didn't see it.

LL: Nobody saw it. Well, they toured it in the Highlands.

Gutter: Because I'm just thinking, given recent political events and given the rise of Nicola Sturgeon and Theresa May, it's a play that's very apt for revival.

LL: Well that's it. It would have been really good to revive it over the past few years.

Gutter: I just want to come back briefly to our cultural relationship with London. The hope for the National Theatre of Scotland was a case of Scotland saying, well, an extension of the old Rebel Inc "Fuck London" mantra. A feeling of "Right, well we'll display our own theatre culture in our own touring theatre company, a national company without walls". Which is a very different way of doing things from most other National Theatres.

LL: That's not quite what has happened though.

Gutter: But is the response to the kind of neglect of aspects of Scottish culture within the rest of the UK, is simply to say

"Okay, we'll do our own thing"? Or should we be more actively trying to make the case for Scottish culture down south, as many in the visual arts have done? Or do you think it's both?

LL: I'd pick both. But I'd certainly hoped that the National Theatre of Scotland would be a bit more of a Communicado Theatre Company writ large, you know, because that suits Scotland's population. And instead of which touring theatre has largely dropped out of...well, no, it hasn't dropped out but you tend to get little arty bits of touring. Touring theatre tends to come from new young theatre companies, experimental stuff. That's not necessarily the best stuff to take to tour to people to get them interested in theatre.

I mean the National Theatre of Scotland has been a very mixed bag, but it's had spectacular successes. I think *Black Watch* is one of the best bits of theatre that's ever, ever been made and I'm very glad. I think it's a great pity that there's a shortage of Scottish people working in the National Theatre of Scotland. It's just a shame, you know. I've nothing against any of the people that do work there. I just wish there were some more Scots, some more people with a Scottish theatrical culture.

Gutter: Because there's a very distinct tradition there, isn't there?

LL: We had a gutsy, rough and ready relationship with variety, you know. I mean, there's something going on like that that's doing it just now, I think, called *Yer Granny*, which to me *doesn't* work because it's denuded of the context in which *it* was written. It's a hunger play. It's a hunger play written about Argentina and just simply setting it in Glasgow – in an unrecognisable Glasgow – and making seventies jokes, doesn't in the end, cut it for me.

Gutter: Right.

LL: It's sort of our musical and what's-its-name past-

Gutter: Music hall, vaudeville?

LL: Our gutsy, upfront, borderline tradition. What I loved about *Black Watch*: it completely was part of a continuum going from 7:84 and Wildcat and touring. And it had great writing by Gregory Burke. It was one of the few things that did, while doing something brand new, plug into the kind of culture that we had. I mean it'll be very interesting to see what Laurie Sansom does, we don't know yet, really. Apart from the big plays which he took to London and were a *huge* hit in London. I would like them to, you know, get some theatre from me and Gerry Mulgrew, you know, because we're not dead yet. Unfortunately, David McLennan *is*. But, you know, the legacy that David has left is firmly going on in Oran Mor. I mean, I've seen some great Oran Mor plays this season and they're not written by people I know. You know, there's a guy called Tim Primrose, did a play called *Broth* which to me was just *fantastic*. It was both crude, funny, musical, upfront, in-your-face and Scottish; and it also had something very profound to say about a very serious subject, which it did with great subtlety. To me, *Broth* did everything that *Yer Granny* didn't, which cost a fortune. And I'm saying that and I'm probably now cutting ties with people that I've worked with very well in the past and hope to work

with again. I loved doing my Scottish *Medea* with Graham McLaren. And that won lots of prizes.

Gutter: And then Babel went, didn't they?

LL: Ah! Babel lost the funding! Typical. Yeah. But their production of *Medea* was great. We could have taken that around the world! And when the National Theatre started, I asked them to revive it at that point with Maureen Beattie while she was still young enough to play *Medea*.

I mean, one of the things- I was in the working party for the National Theatre of Scotland. One of the things that it was meant to do was to celebrate and make possible the further exploitation of some great Scottish theatre from the recent past. I had two pieces that would be considered that. I'm just saying that because it's the truth: of the twenty-four plays I've written, you know, more than half of them are complete duds. But, I have written some good things or some things that were turned – by good theatrical people – into great things. But both *Mary Queen of Scots Got her Head Chopped Off* and *Medea* are great bits of theatre, I would say and they're Scottish too. And the National Theatre of Scotland have only done a very sketchy version of one of my two great plays. I don't feel bitter. But I do think: "Fuck's sake, I would like to see something really great of mine done by the National Theatre of Scotland before I'm deid!"

Gutter: So, do you look back with regret?

LL: I don't think about that, I just get on with working. If I'm doing an Óran Mór,

I'm doing it a hundred per cent, you know and I'm trying to make it as good as I can. And we're trying to make it as good as that play *Broth* – which is only one example of a play that I thought was great this season. There was one that started the season, Butterfly by Anne Hogg, I was heartened to know she's a woman in her late fifties and it's her first play. And it was great! It was two guys on a roof, Paul James Corrigan, I think and the wonderful Frank Gallagher? There were two great Scottish male actors. It was a wonderful play about masculinity, written by a woman and it was her first play. That's just an example of the kind of things that's happening, you know. The other one's written by a guy called Tim Primrose, who I'd never heard of, but I know he's from Edinburgh I would like to hope that the National Theatre of Scotland would be able to gradually hone in to picking up some of the really indigenous stuff that has got that Scottishness to it and exploiting that.

Gutter: But there with the new regime since 2013, do you think the approach will change again?
LL: I don't know. I don't know. I don't know what's going to happen with the arts in Scotland. The National Theatre of Scotland is funded directly by the government and they've got really quite a lot of money. They've got all the budget for theatre in Scotland, really. And it's in the hands of a very few people, few of them Scottish.

Gutter: Where do you stand on popular theatre versus high culture and the ethics of using public money for what is essentially patronage. Óran Mór is a great example of an almost self-sustaining popular lunchtime theatre that is always busy and what David McClellan achieved there is fantastic.

LL: I mean, not all the plays at Óran Mór are great. But you couldn't produce that volume of work in a public funding model – I think they're onto the three hundred and fiftieth play or something. They couldn't all be great, but *some* of them. There were four things I saw last season that I was jealous as anything of, that I wished I'd written.

Gutter: do you think the position for younger writers and artists now is harder than when you were starting out? Or is it much the same?

LL: I don't know, I mean I never applied to the Arts Council for a writing grant to finish anything. You can look at me and say: "Well, you've never had to." And I haven't had to because I've had plays commissioned from theatre companies that have had to do all that work of getting the funding. So I've never been directly funded to do something apart from being the Makar it generally involves going as a freebie to Wester Hailes, to an art thing there, doing one night and contributing to that and enjoying that and writing a poem for the opening of the parliament. It's as varied as that and it's about trying to fight the corner for language, art and creativity in Scotland. And that sounds wanky but that's what I've been trying to do.

Gutter: I'm thinking back to the sixties and seventies when you had poets on telly all the time, you had the likes of Auden and MacNeice and all these people on the radio. Do other things fill the cultural space that poetry once held?

LL: Oh, the radio's still a great place for poets.

Gutter: Because recorded music is everywhere now, is it taking over that space?

LL: No. I just think all the time it's multiplying in its forms and it's getting bits of life. And a lot of the things I've been saying to you Colin have been sounding pessimistic. I'm not pessimistic about art and artists fighting through or about poets, you know.

Gutter: When I was reviewing my questions last night, I was conscious of many of them sounding quite pessimistic, but...

LL: No, I'm not pessimistic. I'm not pessimistic about art or artists because it's a fundamental human whatever. You know, an impulse. It's existed since the cavemen drew aurochs and bison on the walls. We have to make something out of our lives. You know, animals live their lives in the present tense. Artists live in the future and the past as well as the present and they will always continue to do so. Poetry isn't expensive, you know, you just need a biro and a jotter. And there are some good magazines that fight the corner for it

What I would wish for is for funders to start listening to practitioners more and not think of them as pesky moaners. But to listen to what they're saying and say: "How can we take what's sensible out of this?" You know, because what funders must basically want to do is to produce more, in general. That's their raison d'etre. But if we don't watch it can become a situation where all their energy goes into keeping their own jobs and proving what they've done.
And that's a big problem in culture today. Not just in the arts. But a lot of people seem to have to spend a lot of time justifying their work and that's what their work can be, at quite high levels.

Gutter: To me it seems harder for artists to subsist in some ways. But then you said once that: "You don't have a career as a poet, you have a *life* in which you write poems."

LL: Yes, well the poets that went before me: MacCaig, Morgan, they didn't expect to earn a living doing it. I mean, I've never earned a living writing poetry, though I have earned a living out of writing and teaching. I stopped being an art teacher in schools, but I've patched together some sort of living. Sometimes it's been minimal, sometimes, out of writing, you know, and having plays re-produced again. I never expected to earn a bean out of poetry,

I have been able to earn a living as a writer through being a poet and performing poetry. But, you know, the writing of a poem is not going to pay and neither it should. A lot of young writers *want* to be funded before they've written anything. I don't think that's reasonable.

And, you know, there are opportunities and I suppose people should try and find out what the opportunities are but you don't need funding to be a poet, you know, I think that there's an argument that you should have a job and real. You should be able to get some patronage to help you complete things, of course. But not before you've written something.

Gutter: We're in a bit of a paradox where poetry seems in a secular world to be ever more important to people, and anthologies sell well, but collections don't sell much at all. Why do you think that is?

LL: Well, they're expensive and a lot of collections of poetry are too abstruse for readers. And I'm not blaming people for writing them – I don't think people are writing them to *be* abstruse but an awful lot of art *has* become self-referential. Popular stuff is selling in different ways, whether it's on records. But poetry it doesn't have to cost a lot of money.

Gutter: Do you think that there's no place for difficult poetry anymore?

LL: There is a place for difficult poetry, of course there is. But, it's also not reasonable to expect people on the dole to buy it, you know. Poets' responsibility is to write to the best of their ability, the best work they can and not to worry at the writing stage as to how well it's communicating to people, far less how well it will sell.

Gutter: I know that you admire poets like MacCaig, like Leonard, like MacNeice, poets that have a real drive and a flair for language, but also poets who are quite, almost forensic in their rigour to their writing. What is it for you that underpins stuff that really works for you?

LL: If I can hear their voice from the page, often before understanding.

Gutter: Even if you've never heard them perform?

LL: Uh-huh, oh aye, yeah, yeah. I mean, I never heard Lowell perform, but the first time I read a Robert Lowell poem

– and I didn't understand it completely – I loved the sound of it from the page. So... Yes, because a lot of the people that I've still to read and enjoy are dead, so I won't be able to hear them! But, no, I think it's an ever-replenishing stream.

Gutter: It's been four years now, that you've been Makar and you said previously, that your mission was to fight the corner for poetry, so, how do you feel the battle is going?

LL: I've not found it a battle. It's not a battle: people *want* poetry. People want and need poetry. People want truth from the language in their lives. No, it's been wonderful. Personally for me, it's been a life-saver and it's been a privilege to be able to try and do my best for. But I think the next battle that I want to pick up is the one about the teaching of poetry in schools. Because I think something's happened in teaching – in the structures of teaching from above – that is stopping the kind of teaching of literature that should be happening. I was at a friend's – there was a thing on the table, his son's in fourth year and there was this poem on the table – *the poem* they were doing *this term* – and notes all over it, you know, every single word.

I don't think anybody had bothered about the *flow* or the overall meaning. They'd just turned it into a set of problems. I saw, after the title – which was one of those, you know, the first line of the poem is the title, an old, old, technique – but at the end of it, it said: "Caesura" And it isn't a caesura!

It was just the fact that they're getting taught technical terms. It's not the right thing to do, to teach people complicated technical terms first – but it's certainly not the right thing to do teach them wrong! I mean, you only need to know what a caesura is once you're a working poet and you're writing or whatever. Just made me furious: that that's the first thing they would say about the poem, not what does it mean but an absolutely inaccurate identification of a caesura.

It drives me insane that kind of stuff, that and English teachers that haven't read anything themselves. They're now beginning to come through, the product of that, they've only read the things that they had to read in school.

Gutter: But wasn't the advantage of the Scottish curriculum the fact that teachers could select their own texts? What's gone wrong?

LL: I don't know. Maybe they still select their own texts, but the system under which they do it is for one text for the whole term and they're asked to – by the parents as well as by the school – to make people pass the exam. It must be incredibly boring to mark exams nowadays because there's just this set of bullshit answers. And the most important thing to do with poetry, in a school is to have somebody – coming home, as my sister said to me when she was about twelve, I'm ten years older than she is, she said: "We got this lovely poem today, Adelstrop." And she said, Adelstrop to me, who'd never heard of it, as it happens, I was twenty-two at the time, and she said this, and she'd loved it and I'd loved hearing it. And that's what teaching poetry is: giving you the gift of more poems.

Gutter: Going back to the oral tradition and passing it on?

LL: Yeah, passing it on. Instead of which, turning a poem into a terrible problem to be cracked like a- It's not an equation! I get asked all these questions when people are reading things and to mis-readings of lines and you sort of think, you know- It's like, a long, long, while ago this boy said to me: "We were doing this poem a few years ago about a bull and I said it was about a bull and I was told it was not about a bull, I was told it was about sex and whatever and whatever." And he said: "What is it about?" And I said: "A bull." And I said: "It's about some of these other things too."

Gutter: Yeah. There's a battle to roll back that kind of attitude to literature that's been going on probably for, I don't know, thirty years, now? Twenty, thirty years now, maybe?

LL: Thirty, could be thirty, I guess. Terrible, isn't it? But, it's not terrible, because *of course* people are writing, of course things are happening. You know, I'm definitely the opposite of pessimistic.

Gutter: I'll just finish off by talking a wee bit about language and Scots in particular. I mean, for me and for a lot of Scots people who grew up in – I suppose in the state education system – poems like *Kidspoem/Bairnsang* encapsulate the vocal schizophrenia that we all grew up with...
LL: Yeah, and that was written to encourage people to – all over Britain – to keep writing in hometown English, you know.

Gutter: Last week I went to Creative Scotland's launch of their Scots Language

Policy. To be honest, I was encouraged because it was an event I never thought I would see. And there was this document they gave us...

LL: Oh, really, I must get one!

Gutter: I know. You weren't there, so I brought you one.

LL: Oh thank you. I would really love to have gone to that.

Gutter: ...the document was a bit short on specifics but long on aspiration. There was quite a lot of love in the room. If it were up to you, how would you breathe new life into Scots?

LL: Just accept that it's changing all the time, as language does. And celebrate the old stuff when we find it, naturally. You know, don't be ersatz about it.

Gutter: To me, growing up in a mixed Scots and English speaking household, there was always a distinction between the two. If you look at it from a purely linguistics point of view there are enough characteristics to label it a separate language. It fails the mutual intelligibility test even more so than Swedish and Danish would do.

LL: See, I don't think it is a *separate* language. I don't. I think it's a spectrum of languages. I mean Tom Leonard said it brilliantly in that thing he wrote...

Gutter: "All livin language is sacred fuck thi lotha thim"?

LL: No, not that. *Honest* – that thing he wrote called *Honest* – which says: "I don't say 'Yi goan doon the road?' And somebody says to me 'What?' And you say 'Are you going down the road?' You don't say 'That's not what you said the first time!'" You know, sometimes we use one, sometimes

we use the other. No, I think this is terrible.

Gutter: But you get that anywhere, two ways of speaking. Look at the example of Norway where they had their two different forms of Norwegian and then after World War Two they made Nynorsk the official language, because it was the 'demotic' way of speaking. Maybe Scots is too far down the road, too decayed? But I was at an event at the Boswell Book Festival last year, and I learned that Boswell, around the time that Johnson was composing his English dictionary, Boswell was composing a Scots dictionary. Which got 'lost' in a library in Oxford and recently found again. It's about politics and access to power as much as anything.

LL: Really?

Gutter: There are letters from Boswell talking about the death of Scots, even back then. But it's still here and kicking along in certain places. I'm conscious that there's a tension within Scottish writing that kind of mirrors the national confusion. We've got this cultural asset, this treasure trove of words and idiom that, for me, from my Ayrshire background is a distinct way of looking at the world. And it's danger of vanishing. If this was some indigenous language of some Brazilian tribe or something like that we'd be fighting to preserve it. But different writers within Scotland have completely polar attitudes to what we do with it. How do we *preserve* the idiom? How do we do that without fossilising it, without creating some type of newspeak?

LL: Well, I think documents like this are fossilising it. The Scots in here is antique, I don't speak like that.

Gutter: But doesn't everyone have that internal colonist, that cultural cringe about Scots?

LL: Well, I have a cultural cringe about this! "We will shape our work to support and develop Scots language... four key functions of Funding, Advocacy, Development and Influence." How exactly will that help writers and artists to do their work?

Gutter: That's the way public sector managers work, they're been trained in buzzwords. You get the same in the Health service. I really worry that we'll lose proper the Scots idiom that my Dad and Papa used, in a few years all we'll be left with is "jings", "wheesht" and "gie it laldy" and that'll be it, you know. Because people's knowledge of this resource is dying out.

LL: Well, how we would do that is encourage more Burns to be read, to be accessed from the BBC's brilliant archive, where they've got every word that Burns wrote spoken out loud. They didnae really work very hard with the actors on how they pronounced things, they just left it to people. You know, but things are pronounced differently in different areas. Somebody told me they came from a place where they didnae watch "Doctor Who", they watched "Doctor Whae". And I would never say 'whae'. I would say 'wha'. Some of this will die out, but not the great stuff,

Gutter: Is that not the problem, we all come from a slightly different homespeak? So when we see somebody else rendering it in a different way it makes our toes curl.

LL: And there are lots of different speeches and they all make up Scots. You know, they made up Lallans at one point, you know, which was a synthetic language.

LL (referring to Scots Language Policy booklet): Look, it says here: "Scots in our operations: We will accep onie communication as weel as applications for siller support, in Scots." My fear is with that that people will just put their forms in Scots so as a certain amount of Scots things will get ticked.

Gutter: At the magazine we get quite a lot of writing in Scots and a lot of it's not up to scratch.

LL: Most of it isn't.

Gutter: So what do you advise, say, young writers, new writers, I mean, should they dive into the old dictionaries like MacDiarmid did?

LL: If they want, they should do that! But not write Scots language policy application prose! We all understand English.

Gutter: Okay, maybe that rendering of it is wrong. But if you're a Cockney and you came up to Glasgow you would struggle to understand. You would fail the mutual intelligibility test, which most linguists view as the test of what's a language and what's a dialect.

LL: Yeah, but they don't feel that they need to have arts policy documents written in Cockney.

Gutter: Robert MacClellan said about *Jamie the Saxt*, he felt Scots only really worked in a historical context for him.

LL: Well, that was true for him. Certainly I wrote *Mary Queen of Scots Got*

Her Head Chopped Off in a *different Scots* from the Scots, arguably still Scots, in which I wrote *Misery Guts*, which was set in the present.

Gutter: There were linguistic anachronisms in *Mary Queen of Scots* as well, you were quite free with your Scots timelines in that.

LL: Yeah, I am. Well, Shakespeare didnae write *Julius Caesar* in Latin, you know. It was Elizabethan English. It was his language. You write in your language.

Gutter: Right! The speech I learned at primary school, I don't use it anymore. In my day-to-day work, I can't use it, because people will make value judgements about my ability if I don't 'talk properly'. But I recognise it's valuable and now I've forgotten most of it – how do I preserve it?

LL: Write fiction. Write fiction, write plays, write poetry. Write characters that do use it. Write. To me the function of language is communication. This document does not further communication. So, therefore, it fails at that level, for me. And I'd be willing to talk about that to somebody. Management speak Scots-ified, antiquely Scots-ified, does not make it less management speak. I'm happy to say that. How do you keep it alive? By using it.

Gutter: But does it not need some sort of validation, because part of the reason I can't use it in day-to-day work is because of other people's ingrained value judgements that it is somehow inferior to English as a way of communication. The only way you move it away from that is to officially validate it.

LL: The validation is by doing it well.

Documents like this make me cringe.

Gutter: Aye, it makes me unhappy too. Doesn't reflect the optimism, the *voice*, that was at the launch.

LL: "Scots Leid Policie." – The 'leid' means the language. Well, I've never used that.

Gutter: "Leid" is a Lallans word, I think. It's a synthetic word. I've prefer 'tung'. I would use tung before anything. Has the same root meaning as the 'langue' in 'language'.

LL: "Policie" – with a capital I-E, that only makes it look like the language of Mary Queen of Scots.

Gutter: I would have used a compound phrase like: 'The Wey Furrit fir Scots'. Scots is direct, Germanic in that way compared to English. 'Policie' is Old French, not sure it is ever made it into Scots.

LL: See, I keep reading that as "Scots Leid Police"! You see?

Gutter: [Laughing] Can I borrow that?

LL: Uh-huh. Because you do look for that and whatever. See? [INDICATES PHOTO IN BOOKLET] *Tam O Shanter* by Communicado Theatre Company. Fantastic! Well, fund that! That's how you keep it alive, do it well.

Gutter: the word 'dialect' annoys me because it implies a power-relationship to some non-existent orthodox language.

LL: That some people speak properly and other people don't.

LL: I mean, I always quote Tom Leonard in *Situations, theoretical and contemporary* "And the prisons were full of many voices. But never the dialect of the judges." You know, RP's just a dialect! I don't mind 'dialect' if what it says is: "Distinct voice." But I'd prefer to lose the word because it has been used to marginalise over the years, so: 'voice'. I will use the word 'voice'. Or 'tung'. 'Tung', I quite like 'tung'. 'Tongue' – but I'd like to get the ears into it as well.

Gutter: Aye. Lugs!

LL: [FLICKING THROUGH BOOKLET] The Kelpies are beautiful. I mean there's great art in Scotland. What does it all mean? "Quo life, the warld is mine/The floo'ers and trees they're a' my ain./I am the day in the sunshine/Quo life, the warld is mine." [INDICATES PICTURE] Ron 'Makar' Butlin. Edwin Morgan hated the word 'Makar' by the way, we should say that.

Gutter: Did he?

LL: Yes. He thought it was antique. I don't mind teaching somebody a new word, because the meaning of it's quite nice, it's just 'maker'. So I don't mind it. But I do have to say, when I'm anywhere else, or when I'm in Scotland – I have to say to Scottish people, I'm the Scots… which is inaccurate, I'm not the Scots Makar because that insinuates that I write in Scots… I say I'm Scotland's Makar, or the National Poet of Scotland.

Gutter: So are you doing it for a fixed term?

LL: Five years, another six months to go. So they'll be thinking about the next one.

Gutter: What are your plans for after?

LL: Oh, to keep writing! Absolutely to keep writing and to keep profiting from the higher profile it's given me and to keep gigging and get more things going.

Gutter: Anything you'd like to have done as Makar that you didnae get the chance to do?

LL: Well, so far, I haven't gone to a lot of schools and I want to do that. Maybe at the very end of my term, because I wouldnae have had time before. There's always wee things, you should see my diary it's bonkers, you know. It's not all Makar stuff, but it's things that have grown out of being the Makar.

Gutter: What's next for you, writing-wise?

LL: Oh, I'm writing two plays. Both of them I'm writing really kind of up against the wall. One of them I've got time to write, but the other one I applied for, well, I wrote speculatively – something for people to put a document in to apply for funding. We found out at the very end of April we've got the funding. It goes into rehearsal on August 16th. Luckily I'd written it speculatively, mostly, during the year, because the Director kept saying to me: "Liz, I think we'll get this." And I got the gift of a day with some actors. That was from a thing called Playwrights Studio Scotland. And I will, eventually, once people at the theatre company do the paperwork, get a proper commission to write it and all that. But there would have been no time for me to write it had we waited to hear from Creative Scotland. They don't actually factor that in. They've got to give you the information. It's exactly like saying to an architect: "You go onsite on Monday", and they haven't yet done the drawings.

Gutter: Are you looking forward to having more time after Makardom?

LL: I'm looking forward to saying 'yes' to *only* the things I want to do for myself. But that probably won't be that different. I hope. I would like to go round some schools because I would like to read them poetry, my own and other people's. And tell them that there's no point to it, and tell teachers not to teach people about caesuras. Especially when they don't know what one is! Give them poems, for the reason you read poems: for joy and life. Poetry's about joy and life. It's about the same thing that a song is. It's not to get you through an exam and never read another poem in your life again. So, I would like to do some schools, because I think I can show kids that you do it for fun, not for exams. I'll have to find some funding though because I cannae afford to do it myself and it's exhausting. You're really *on*.

Gutter: It's a performance.

LL: Exactly. So, I would have to be getting, proper rates and my travel expenses. But you know, I'm cheap! I've got a senior rail pass and I've got a bus pass, so very cheap.

Gutter: What are your two plays? Are you allowed to tell me?

LL: Yes, yes! Well, one of them's nearly written, too. That's the thing, I've got three scenes to write of that before August. I know what they are, but I havenae got a day to do it!

Gutter: Are you back to the classics again, or are you...?

LL: No, in a way this play is about a couple. It's called *What goes around*. And it starts off with an actor and an actress who have just done the read-through of *La Ronde*. You know that play that's got a soldier and a prostitute, then the next one the soldier and his girlfriend and a maid. Then there's the maid and the young gentleman of the house, there's the young gentleman of the house and a young married lady, there's the married lady and her husband, then there's the husband and a young girl, then there's the young girl and a poet, then there's a poet, dramatist and an actress, then there's the actress and a count, then there's the count and the first prostitute.

Gutter: It comes all the way back?

LL: Yes. So this does as well with this couple, the actor and actress. I also should've said the other big thing at the end of the Makar, is that I'm getting another collection together.

Gutter: With Polygon again?

LL: Yeah, hopefully with Polygon. I hope so. Part of the Makar's job is that you get support for the publication of the book. And well, I've got more than enough work to go in it.

Gutter: Aye, absolutely.

LL: It's a long while since my last collection. It's a long while since *The Colour of Black and White*. It's going to be a mixture, it'll have both the entertainments and the other stuff in it. But then Burns did that. He put in, you know, songs as well as poems and filth among the other stuff. I'll have to put them in shape as well, I'll be doing that in the autumn. But I've got the second act, mostly, of my big Moliere play and I need to have that by September.

Gutter: When's that going to be produced?

LL: Next May. In rehearsal next April.

THEPOETRYSOCIETY

Presents

National Poetry Competition

Judges: Sarah Howe
Esther Morgan
David Wheatley
Deadline: 31 October 2015

First prize: £5000
Second prize: £2000
Third prize: £1000
Commendations: £200

It's easy to enter online at www.poetrysociety.org.uk/npc
or call us on 020 7420 9880 for more information

Soondscapes

Christine De Luca

I da dizzied hoose, a strum o flechs baet
endless drums fornenst a frenzied window.
Belligerent, dey want nedder in nor oot.

Apö da broo, ahint a wheeshtit chapel,
twa windmills spin new soondscapes owre
da laand, kert-wheelin alleluias.

Cloistert granite hadds a orchestration
o birds, a oorie whirr, a vimmerin
o whaaps an peewits. Da wind

troo da grind is a spaekin in tongues
wi da bruckit feed-hoop tunin in:
idder-wirldly, intimately insistent.

Aa dis music ta lö tae, ta slip inta:
a aald organ nönin, a hushie hubbelskyu.
Up owre da hill, airms turn, da haert lifts.

Soundscapes

In the dizzied house, a strum o flies beat
endless drums against a frenzied window.
Belligerent, they want neither in nor out.

On the brow of the hill, behind a silent chapel,
two windmills spin new soundscapes over
the land, cart-wheeling alleluias.

Cloistered granite holds an orchestration
of birds, an eerie whirr, tremulous sounds
of curlew and lapwing. The wind

through the metal gate is a speaking in tongues
with the broken feed-hoop tuning in:
other-worldly, intimately insistent.

All this music to attend to, to slip into:
an old organ droning, an uproarious lullaby.
Up over da hill, arms turn, the heart lifts.

Wirkin tagidder

Christine De Luca

Mi een is aye lived der separate lives:
da richt, da dominant twin – short-sichtit
an foo o hitsel – laerned ta read nae budder;

da left, da lang-sichtit squintin een, wid
switch aff ithoot aksin, refuse ta tak pairt.
Der spent a lifetime at odds wi een anidder,

tellin stories fae different angles, bamboozlin,
confusin da jury. But truth seems ta tak
baith mi een: wan ta speir trowe da lens

da reffel o elements, ta needle da eemages
up clos; da tidder ta fix on da langer view,
sharpen da starns, akse akward questions.

I need baith: shalmillens o da closs-up;
an da enspeeritin wan – a bent for pattren,
for idder wirlds. An whan A'm seekin

licht, lik some uncan craitir blinnd i da djubs
o a cave, I close baith een, live in hoop
o trivvellin dat brittle twa-ply treed o life.

Working together

My eyes have always lived their separate lives:
the right, the dominant twin – short-sighted
and full of itself – learned to read no bother;

the left, the long-sighted squinting one, would
switch off without asking, refuse to take part.
They've spent a lifetime at odds with one another,

telling stories from different angles, bamboozling,
confusing the jury. But truth seems to take
both my eyes: one to research through the lens

the tangle of elements, to needle the images
up close; the other to fix on da longer view,
sharpen the stars, ask awkward questions.

I need both: fragments of the close-up;
and the inspiriting one – a bent for pattern,
for other worlds. And when I'm seeking

light, like some unfamiliar creature blind in the depths
of a cave, I close both eyes, live in hope
of groping for that brittle two-ply thread of life.

Light Show at the Botanics

Christine De Luca

It's November, a feral night
and damply furtive.
Scent of viburnum masks the fox's stink.

The pond is primordial
its soundscape reptilian.
Beams joust, lances tilt.

If we weren't wildly in love already
we would have head-longed
into the moment. Huge flowers drift past.

We are hankering, sublunary creatures
with that marshmallowy moon in our eyes.
Everyone here is Lucy or a lover.

We sway like reeds in the old lily pond.
Out of this zany dark and ice we will carry
longing and the sun in our eyes forever.

An Appointment at The National Library of Scotland

Kate Hendry

What can I show my father, when he comes to stay
with me? Edinburgh – a city he frowns on
for its wealth and power and childhood memories
of Sunday visits to Great Aunt Enid in her villa
near the zoo, the hard chair at the hot bay window

where *(Sit still, keep quiet, wait for mother)*
he picked orange peel from fruitcake.
What can I show him, once the tour is over
of my too small flat, my windowless kitchen?
The view to the Botanics from our dining table?

We'll have no time to sightsee – Thursday morning
before his 12.45 train home. So I offer him
a visit to the Library, as if it's mine.
I know he's tried before; he was told off at the door
for turning up without warning or proper ID.

I know which forms he needs, where the lockers are.
I'll bring a pound coin for his coat and bag,
lend him a pencil, take him to the lift
up to the special collections reading room,
to see notebook drafts of Sorley MacLean's poems.

We'll try to decipher the Gaelic, find 'Hallaig',
(long blu-tacked to my father's bathroom wall).
He'll whisper the first line to me –
'Tha tìm, am fiadh, an coille Hallaig' –
while I stare through crossings out to the words beneath.

A Sleep

Russell Jones

You've taken to bed again, your zimmer
by the window. It's early afternoon,
but winter, and soon the day will disappear.
I sit beside you so we can be near.

The clock, like your heart, still ticks.
Dusk brings your breath with it.
The sun tucks itself away. I don't
turn the light on, but stare

at the silhouette of your frame, mechanical,
like a crane hunched over a derelict city.
You groan. Your feet shuffle in your sleep,
dashing through fields near your old home,

towards the stream where we fished,
picked berries, built kites and box cars.
I pull a blanket over you, put on the heat
and the television, watch repeats

of the old movies you loved.
Garland sings about elsewheres
over rainbows, and in the screen's glow
as you hear her words, your lips follow.

Sylvia

Fran Baillie

Painstakkinly,
oot o er box
thon Boston lassie
selectit
er colours, er words.

Pysonous raid o jarred bell-tulips,
bitter oarange, lang-daid,
faydit yella, jandis-tintit,
seeknin green o envy bred.
Forgit- mi- nut, si cald an loveless
daurkest indigo o deepest hue,
violet quasht si violently
aathin imbued wi cruellest blue.

Shid brush,
nae rush.

Til Infidelity's spectre,
bleakest, blackburd-black
cast its raven shadda,
twistit perspective.

Er landscape cheengt,
became a wystland,
buryin thon rehnbow.

Sestina of the House

Sally Evans

I slid to a halt at the house,
turned the car in the driveway
on the platform above the river
where the trout stream runs down
while I stood breathing memories
and understanding change.

There weren't many changes.
The garden surrounding the house
was well-kept, but in memory
flowers crowded the driveway
and paths where I wandered down
to the cool grass. Time is a river

and this tributary of the river
had a pool. I threw in some change
and watched silver disks drift down
to wish good fortune on the house.
Not ready to drive away
from such rampant memories

or seeds lost in the stones of memory
and now sprouting in the river
of time, I glance down the driveway
wishing this moment never to change.
There is no one in the locked house
and I so early coming down.

I need to tell or write down
these new gifts of memory
sprung from the stone of the house
and joining the full river
of time, in which change
is inevitable. The driveway

is the way there and back, the driveway
links to the road going down
to the motorway interchange,
leaving stories of locked memories
which will leach away to the river
from the secluded house.

So I'll leave the house by the driveway,
let the river calm itself down
as my memories change.

Boy

Stav Poleg

The most unlikely fish,
swimming upright like a street-lamp

in an ocean.
I'd like to say

when I first learned you're a seahorse
everything

fell into place.
How you'd been curled into the circles

of your spine,
breathing bubbles into your paper-cut

slow skin.
I'd like to say I've always understood

the hesitation
of your water-pace,

your cellophane-like fins
    that could be wings,

or once were wings,
    the most unlikely Pegasus.

Once upon a time
there was a seahorse, a yellow seahorse,

a little lemon bubble
like a curl of light and stone.

 But now that my palm
is as flat as the ocean,

I can't seem to hold you,
    I'd follow

your footprints
instead.

The Circus Always Makes me Cry

John Saunders

The lithe girl who checked my ticket stub
is a spinning acrobat in the ceiling of the tent,
her body a marionette she holds with her teeth.

The spotlight silhouettes her sparkling figure,
shows us the sinewy map of her physique
as she swings through her stardom

after which she will sell candy floss
and stack stalls at the end of the show.
She finishes now, takes her bow,
absorbs our grateful applause.

There is so much of my past I don't recall,
those small moments of light that make a child
feel at the centre. I remember the effort,
how praise was a ransom never surrendered.

Holofernes

Stewart Sanderson

Not the poor dupe cringing
before Judith on some black
Renaissance canvas
but that foolish schoolmaster
who fills *Love's Labours Lost*
with macaronic chatter.

I too have often caught
the rich fumes rising
from the feast of languages
and like him tasted
saffron words, syntax
of frangipani
dialects of burnt sugar
on a glass's rim.

And yes, I too have woken
among false friends
head clanging
after another all
nighter in the woods
of sense. Like him I've stolen
retching from the party
only to return more
ravenous than ever.

I too will settle
for the scraps – a bone
to pick, a bowl
to lick clean underneath
the tablecloth.

There's famine
on the Volga of the tongue
and better shanks or trotters
than an empty belly.

Asking
(for her)

RA Davis

if you see her
tell her I was asking for her

as others might say
I was asking *after* her
unleashing a pack of questions
with a scrap of her scent

change the emphasis:
he was asking for *you*
as a deathbed confessor asks
as the coma patient wakes and asks

make it what it is
a summons, a subpoena
a ransom demand
anyway

if you see her
tell her I was asking for her

The Deil's Tell

Wendy Orr

Yer muin's a scourer.
scriven wi strangulwire.
iron as yer blastit bullit
puckert in the waa
ahint yer ain burst heid.
                    Filth.
likes o yer buckit o mulk
bleach afore it turnt pink.
                    Muck.
Ma muin's black as vanish
likes o yon birlt halo a ance
spun oot hie as hell.
Derker yit, efter ma spurnin.
                    Whit?
Ye think the derk's stappin
filth fae fleein lowse?
A telt yese afore.
Derk as filth as muck as muin.
                    It's aw ane.

This country, she thinks, this country where children throw dog mess on people's windows then go home and sleep in their warm beds and their mothers don't ask them where they've been and what they have been doing.

Newhaven
Sinothile Baloyi

Newhaven

Sinothile Baloyi

Violet goes to shove the hoover into the cupboard under the stairs. Then, shocked by her own violence, she puts it away a little more gently – a replacement wouldn't come cheap. She doesn't empty the clear plastic dust receptacle though. That can wait another day.

The cries from upstairs are subsiding. Violet can hear Stephen giving their six year old daughter a telling off. Only days before, she had shut her three year old sister in a cupboard after convincing her it was bigger on the inside, like a Tardis. Who knew what other imaginative forms of cruelty she had come up with?

'Stephen!' she shouts up the stairs, at the institutional-blue bathroom door at the top. Who voluntarily paints their door that colour, she wonders, as she waits for Stephen to respond.

He doesn't. She hates that. She shouts again, and the sound bounces off the bathroom door and back down the stairs at her.

'In a minute!' he replies from the children's bedroom.

All she wants is a 'yes?' She doesn't need him to come down the stairs. Is that so hard?

Violet goes upstairs and into the fire-engine red children's room. Another odd decorating choice their landlord won't let them redress.

Thandi is nestled in her father's lap looking hard done by in her Peppa Pig pyjamas, thumb firmly in mouth, and head tucked into the crook of his arm.

'What's going on?' She's looking at six year old Ella who is jumping up and down on her bed, unruly curls flying everywhere.

'Ella, stop that, right now!' Violet puts on her thunderclap voice. It's the only one Ella responds to.

'I was only joking; she didn't have to get upset about it'. Ella doesn't sound the least bit contrite.

Violet's gaze shifts to Stephen sitting cross legged on Thandi's bed, looking uselessly at Ella.

'I really haven't got time for this, you deal...'

'I WAS dealing with it!' he interrupts in a harassed voice.

Violet sighs.

'Fine. I need to get ready for work. There are a couple of loads of laundry to be done. I haven't got time, so can you do it while I'm out?' She doesn't think she should have to tell him, though experience has taught her it's her best chance of making sure it happens.

'Yeah, sure', he answers.

She walks out of the room to the sound of Stephen's voice, his patient one, no doubt trying to appeal to Ella's better nature. She wonders if six year olds have better natures, better than what?

She knows what he'll do with the girls today, same as every Saturday she works; DVDs and popcorn. Violet doesn't approve, but he claims it's the one day a week he gets to decide what he does with the kids, so she says nothing now.

Violet sits on the top deck of the number 7 Newhaven bus as it trundles up Ferry Road. She looks in the windows of the flats that flank the busy road as the bus makes its way through the Saturday afternoon traffic toward Constitution Street. She wonders why everyone has house plants in their homes. Everyone she knows, as well as the anonymous people whose windows she is looking through, has house plants. She has no house plants. She has two children and a husband instead. Of course her husband doesn't need her for survival, but she imagines him choking in a man-high gunk of hoover dust, his long neck poking out above the top like a giraffe. Definitely no time for a house plant.

She is still pondering the house plant question as she ties her apron on. Violet works in an Indian restaurant on Hanover Street on Saturday afternoons and three nights during the week. She hates it there. The Bangladeshi chef once told her, innocent as you like, that all black women are whores. 'You go to London and you go to King's Cross and you see them on the street'. He seemed to regard it as a simple statement of fact, and looked at Violet as though expecting her to back up his story. She had looked incredulously at his brown laughing eyes, and wondered if he was colour blind, or just plain nasty.

This was a few weeks ago, and Violet has been looking for another job ever since. And now her boss, the restaurant owner, thinks she has an attitude problem because she finds it hard to smile. He does not want her to work out front anymore, so she spends more time in the kitchen now. Peel some onions, wash the pots, and when that's done, chop up the salad and watch the racist chef cook delicious Bangladeshi curries. No false smiles required.

The restaurant owner likes to think he is a benevolent man – a social revolutionary even. Violet imagines that's how he explains paying his staff cash in hand, saving them from paying tax to 'the man'. He asks Violet if she'd like to earn some extra money by going over to help his wife with the domestic chores at their house in Trinity when the restaurant is quiet. Violet clenches and unclenches her left hand once and forcing her voice to sound normal, politely declines. Now he really is convinced she has an attitude problem.

At five o'clock, after prepping vegetables for the dinner service, she takes her apron off. She smells of curry, spices and cooking. She doesn't mind too much, but she is looking forward to having a shower. She wonders if Stephen took the kids to the park or even got them dressed. When he doesn't get them dressed, because he cannot be bothered, he says they were having a 'pyjama day' as though that's the same thing as sports day.

Violet decides she is not going to have an argument tonight. It's been a busy day and she hasn't got the energy. Also, she knows that if they do, he will end up crying. She hates that. Violet doesn't think men should cry. Stephen cries hot angry tears when he gets frustrated that things are not going the way he wants them to. Violet suspects that he knows that the cracks that are forming are getting wider and deeper every day, and that he can't fix them. The cracks do their most prolific growth in the three nights a week that she works. That is when they pass each other in the hall way. Hello. goodbye. hope work goes okay. hope work went okay.

When he isn't looking, she watches him quietly, looks at his soft reddish lips, almost childlike in their fullness. She thinks of the warm squishy 'mwuah!' kisses he gives. Not so often now. They are more likely to be chewing something crunchy – leftover salad eaten out of the bowl, a stick of celery, granny smith apples. She hates those apples. When she's eaten them in the past they've made the air blowing into her mouth rub against her teeth. She didn't need to know that she was breathing. To be alive was proof enough thank you.

She looks at him and thinks of his smooth pink, almost hairless, naked body. Warm. Always warmer than hers. Then she stops, embarrassed and shy at her thoughts. Lately they don't have sex. She thinks that if they do he will forget that they have problems. She doesn't want him to forget that. He says she uses sex as a stick to beat him with. She says that is ridiculous. Violet cannot understand how he can want to have sex when they can't even have a decent conversation about anything.

An hour and a half after she gets home, the children are bathed and in fresh pyjamas. She kisses both of them goodnight, and goes into the tiny baby wash scented bathroom for a shower. Violet stands under the hot shower. She could stand here forever, she thinks, as the hot water trickles down her back in a hot stream of pleasure. She smiles to herself. She has a nail brush and is scrubbing at her finger nails to get the onion smell out of her hands. Next, she lifts her foot onto the edge of the bath and scrubs at the hard skin there with a grey pumice stone. So much hardness and smell to get at.

Afterwards, she sits in the living room and puts the TV on. Stephen has gone out while she was in the shower. She knows where he is – the pub at the bottom of the road. She sits in the glow of the TV screen, and flicks from one channel to another looking for something to hold her attention. There is nothing. She thinks of calling her sister. She checks the time and that she has enough credit before dialling. The phone rings and rings.

Violet goes to check on the sleeping children and comes back to the living room. A movie about a middle aged man who falls in love with one of his students, played by Penelope Cruz, is starting in fifteen minutes. She decides she will watch that, and will make some tea before it starts.

The kitchen window looks out onto a scruffy bit of turf across the narrow street. Short green metal railings with peeling paint enclose it. White lettering on a dark green sign next to the entrance proclaims the sorry looking piece of ground a park.

A man in a green and white tracksuit top walks past a small group of boys – a seemingly permanent fixture – past the dog mess bin that sits at the entrance, and turns left towards the city centre. Violet turns her back to the window, picks up the kettle, and stands filling it at the tap.

She hears the thud before she sees anything, and for a minute looks around the kitchen confused. Another thud and she looks over her shoulder at the window. That's when she sees it sliding slowly down against the window pane. The black plastic bag gets caught on the window sill, and the whole thing slithers to a disgusting halt. She runs to her children's room upstairs and looks out from behind the curtain – there's no sign of the boys now. They must have seen her put the light on in the kitchen and seized their opportunity. She can hear her heart beat in her ears, the angry hot blood coursing through her veins. This country, she thinks, this country where children throw dog mess on people's windows then go home and sleep in their warm beds and their mothers don't ask them where they've been and what they have been doing. At least it's not eggs this time; they are harder to wash off.

Violet gets a roll of kitchen towel, yellow gloves and a bin bag. She fills a bucket with water, and mixes in a bottle cap full of bleach. She locks the door on her sleeping children and walks round the side of the house to her kitchen window.

When she gets back inside she can't get the smell of dog excrement and bleach out of her nose, and feels that no matter how careful she's been, she must have got some on her clothes and skin. She takes off all her clothes, puts them in the washing machine, and goes into the shower, this time scrubbing her skin almost raw with her exfoliating gloves.

Clean again, she checks on her sleeping daughters before going back to the living room where the TV is still on. She has only missed ten minutes of the movie.

Auld An Yung

Hamish Scott

The auld man is leanin on his bed, aa bien an lown, whan he tents the streekin, forcie staps o the wee lassie stertin tae speel the stair. He souchs wi jalousin the bairn is cumin for tae see hir gutcher an bringin an en tae his rest. The bairn is back fae the Sunday Schuil the noo an hir mither, that brocht hir hame, is straucht tae hir hoose-wark again. Wi hir faither awa an nane o hir freens aroon, that leas hir wi hir gutcher. He's kinna hoose-tied lik hir mither but wi be-in unable wi the pains. Tae the bairn, tho this maks him a bit crabbit an ill-willie, it maks him rife wi time an aa an thus for ornar apen tae hir.

The bairn reaks the heid o the stair an, tho hir staps noo dackle, the auld man leuks tae his chaumer door an waits on the bairn kythin, graithin tae smile at hir for tae smore his spite at hir cumin. Certie, suin the door is huilie apenin a wee an the bairn's blate face teetin roon it. Finnin hir gutcher smuein at hir, hir leuk turns tae a muckle smirk, for it shaws he's as bowsum tae hir as he iver wis. She pits the door wide tae the waa an crouse stends up tae him, haudin hir Bible yit.

'Whit ye daein gutcher?' she speirs at him.

'A'm haein a rest,' he replies. 'Whit wis ye lairnt the day than?' he asks at hir tite as he leuks an nods tae hir Bible. He for ornar canna be daein wi kirk maiters but sae lang as him an the bairn is haein a crack insteid o a play he's no carin, for he can least be restin his bouk sum.

The bairn streeks hirsel hie wi hir pride at hir new ken: 'Aa aboot a auld man cryed Noah an his faimlie, that biggit thairsel a muckle bait cryed a Ark, again a gret muckle fluid owre the hail warld, an pit twa o ilka beast in it, an tentit thaim aa or the water gaed doon an thai cud lan' – than hir wirds devals an hir een lichts up wi a thocht that cums tae hir juist: 'A ken!' she declares, 'you'll can be Noah wi his Ark an A'll can be yer grandochter that helps ye wi tentin the beas!'

The auld man hidlins souchs tae hissel at his prattick misfarin – an that quick. Noo he hunkers hissel tae haein a play wi the bairn, for he can tell she's that kittelt up wi hir notion she'll no be bringin an en tae *that*. He smues at the bairn again: 'Okay than, ma bed is ma Ark. C'wa on buird!'

As hir gutcher warsles tae sit up, the bairn smiles at hirsel wi anither muckle smirk an, pittin hir Bible aside, scrauchles snell upon his bed. Hir gutcher's birr micht be pitten-on sum but while he's playin wi hir she's no carin.

'Cum on Noah,' she crys on hir gutcher sae suin as abuird the Ark, 'lat's git tentin the beas for thai'l no be daein that thairsel!'

Noo sittin up, the auld man hidlins souchs tae hissel aince mair afore settin on wi the bairn.

Auld an yung suin sattles intae thair play. The bairn haes hir gutcher feedin, waterin an exerceisin sinnrie perrs o beas efter ither – tae him for an iverlestin – an gin he slacks ava she aye hauds at him. He's daein the muckle feck o the wark an, i maugre o thair ages an sibness, is sumwey unable for shiftin wi hir – an *she* is supposed tae be helpin *him!* 'Whit a beas the bairn kens,' the gutcher tells hissel thrawnlie, 'an she's a naitral maistress forby.'

Wi ilka new perr o beas he's tentin, the mair the gutcher is wantin his rest. Throu time, he canna thole it onie mair. He haes a leuk aboot hissel for sumthing that can git him easement. Seein the bairn's Bible, he straucht kens it's whit he's efter. As he raxes for it, in a glint he thinks on a wey o uisin it.

'Leuk!' he declares, 'here a beuk on the tentin o beas. A'll better see it.'

'But whit o tentin oor beas the noo?' the bairn asks at the auld man while leukin misgien at his wird.

'Ye maun be daein it yer lane,' he rebats wi, 'seein as hoo A'l be in hauns wi this beuk,' an he begins leukin thrang wi the bairn's Bible.

The auld man noo rests, in a mainer, upon the apen pages o the bairn's Bible while lattin on he's readin it eident. This is a hantle better for him, an he haes anerlie whiles tae speak a wird tae the bairn anent the tentin o beas, as gif he is referrin tae whit he is readin, for tae haud his new place i the play.

Meantime, the bairn is tentin the beas, but it's no the same thing ava aa hir lane seemin, an hir gutcher is set on misgiein hir. Throu time, gittin stawed wi sic play, she decides tae gang back doon the stair an fin hirsel sumthing ense tae dae.

'A maun awa noo,' she annunces tae hir gutcher while scrammlin aff o the bed. 'See an tent the beas for us,' she adds as she leas the chaumer.

'Ay,' hechts the gutcher while leukin up at hir fae his beuk an shapin tae kythe disappyntit at hir gaun.

As he sits thare tho, insteid o tentin the beas, he tents the staps o the bairn as she gaes clampin doon the stair. Whan the staps deval thai ir follaed wi the soun o a door apenin than steekin. The auld man souchs wi relief, for at lang lenth the bairn is gaen an the play is owre. Noo he can git a ly an rest hail aince mair. Layin the Bible aside, he lys back doon upon his lair.

Hooaniver, the auld man canna git sattelt richt, for noo he rues his wey wi the bairn, for be-in ill-willie an twa-fauld tae the wee thing – whit wi misuisin hir Bible an aa.

An he mynds she mou'd Noah wis nine hunner year auld. Leevin the same, at his age noo he wad be yung yit an, i proportion, kinna ages wi the lassie – a sort o bairn hissel.

Enchanted Forest

Stephanie Brown

Laura sat at the table, smoking in her dressing gown in a way she had sworn she never would. She watched the smoke accumulate around her daughter's head.

Aoife was snorting cereal milk out through her nose, making patterns on the table.

'Mummy, Cat says you're like a dragon. Always puffing away, smoking up the place and making it stink...'

'Is that right, munchkin.'

Every kid has an imaginary friend, don't they? Laura had one called Billy Bob who would tell her she didn't have to have baths. Any time a bath was suggested she'd pipe up with total authority – sorry, can't, Billy Bob says no. But then she'd pretty much known that Billy Bob was an invention. Aoife really didn't know.

Niall had stocked up on leaflets because of the many behaviours Aoife displayed even as a toddler that were 'not normal,' so he had the perfect one to hand for when she drew a giant, bloody penis in felt tip pen on her bedroom wall. Laura could really have torn him a new one and pretty much did for suggesting there was anything wrong with their sweet, kooky little girl. She remembered, quite clearly, drawing a freaky-looking skull with mucous all over it in primary school and getting in deep trouble for it, but she only did it because she thought it looked cool, and what was all this pathologizing of childhood anyway? So what if she thinks a giant cat lives in her bedroom? So what if she lets the cat take the blame for some of the weird things she does?

'Hey, Fifi, why'd you draw a big willy on your wall?' she'd asked her, quite casually. Aoife looked sheepish and then burst into tears.

'I didn't even want to! Cat made me do it!' She cupped Laura's ear and whispered sticky tears into it: 'Cat tries to make me bad.'

'But Cat just lives inside your head really, doesn't she? She isn't really real like us, so you don't have to do what she says.'

'Well, I think she is real... But no-one except me can see her.' Aoife shrugged in exasperation, because it is just so hard to be magical sometimes. 'She's out there playing on the swings right now.' Laura had actually turned around to stare at the empty swing set outside, blowing in the breeze.

'Look, we have to deal with this,' Niall had said. He held her by both shoulders and looked her in the eyes, as if to hypnotise her into acceptance. 'She's taken this whole thing too far now. The other kids at school even know about it! They don't want to play with her because they think she's creepy!'

'You're a fucking reptilian,' Laura had said, but she still loved that cold-blooded bastard. She loved his way of grabbing things by the balls, of knowing how to deal with every situation like a good person should. But it was only now that she knew this, smoking at the breakfast table with a legally binding separation agreement before her which was dog-eared and covered in ash because she could never bring herself to do anything but pick at its edges and stare at it.

She tried to read it, but all she could read was the story of her own infidelity. She couldn't take it in. She read in it the sound of lips on lips, the smell of sweat and sex, and it made her gag. When asked by friends why she'd done it, she couldn't explain other than to say it was some irresistible compulsion to be bad that arose from stress and misery, like making things worse would somehow be better than things remaining the same.

Niall hadn't responded like a reptilian then, and she wondered if that was what she'd wanted after all. Tears dripped from the end of his nose, and she knew that he felt just like she did. But it was too late because Niall wasn't the type of person to fight a losing battle. He would sweep up his tears and gather himself. He would go and be with the other good people out there in the good, good world.

Sometimes Laura understood Cat perfectly. Sleeping with a colleague you weren't even attracted to was somehow like drawing a giant penis on the wall, sprouting with fat and obscene pubic hairs. Sometimes you just had to vomit out the shit.

Now, Aoife was staring intently at something non-existent in the kitchen corner and Laura had long-since stopped pretending that she was fine. She heard things, she saw things, and they were becoming more and more frightening to her. She was too old for imaginary friends anyway and did strange things like touch mirrors to see if her finger would go right through. She was so smart and funny and observant and Laura wanted to shake her when she did these things, because she just couldn't understand how you could be so smart and not see what's real and what's not.

Dr Morrison had told her that this wasn't how to deal with things, but obviously it didn't need to be said. She wasn't a fucking moron. Ever since she'd come to understand how ill her daughter was, Laura felt a constriction around her chest and throat that didn't let up at any time of the day or night. No matter what she was thinking, underneath that thought she was really thinking of her daughter doped up and drooling on Thorazine, growing up into someone who walks around in a muumuu and awaits the rapture. No thought was too crazy; nothing was impossible. Her beautiful, button-nosed daughter was utterly, utterly at the mercy of her own mind.

Today involved another trip to see Dr Morrison, and she would have to tell her that Aoife was not doing well. She would suggest increasing her medication, and she would feel guilty, because there were no studies to say what these drugs, designed for adults, could do to the pliable brain of a kid. No matter what they told her, Laura cherished the hope that somehow this disease would go away as Aoife grew. She pictured impossible things like her daughter graduating from university or working in a bank; living boringly and happily. It was too much to imagine great heights so she kept her ambitions small.

Laura had smoked three cigarettes and dropped the butts into the scum of her coffee. Aoife had lapsed into a very weird silence, and was staring, open-mouthed, at nothing.

'What's going on, hon?' Aoife didn't answer, this being the worst of it, when she was so engrossed in her hallucinations she hardly registered the real world. They were going to be late and Laura jiggled her leg, knowing that she still had to fight the demons of the netherworld to get Aoife into the car as well as sign this fucking thing. Which was now hardly legible, it was covered in so many coffee stains. Maybe she'd have to request a new one, she thought, curling the edge once again. But then, with a flourish, her hand simply picked up the pen and signed it.

There would be time for histrionics later. Now, they had to not miss this appointment because they wouldn't get another one for months probably and the G.P. wouldn't mess with her prescription because he didn't understand a single fucking thing about what was going on.

While Aoife sat transfixed at the kitchen table, Laura climbed into jeans and ran a brush through her hair, choking on her own saliva momentarily when the memory of Evan's fingers surfaced, à propos of nothing. They had hard, flat pads at the end from playing guitar. They were like frog toes, with suckers. She brushed her hair as if to brush them out of the tangle, then hussled Aoife out of her chair and into a jacket.

'Right, then. You ready?' Aoife said nothing, didn't even nod. She took her hand, leading her to the car, careful to pick up the much accidentally-on-purpose forgotten separation document.

As soon as they started moving, Aoife piped up.

'Are we going to Daddy's?' This was turning into a recurring refrain of hers, a depressingly predictable one too. They could have been in some crappy 'feelgood' movie about a family who are obviously going to get back together once a friendly and real giant cat pops out the wardrobe to save the day. *Hey, it's OK, your daughter's not crazy, I'm a real cat!*

'Sorry, honey. We have to go to the hospital again.' Aoife shook her head and put her fingers in her ears.

'Mummy, Cat says you're evil.'

Laura's veins pulsed. She looked at her daughter in the rear-view mirror. The proper response would be to ask why, but she didn't.

'Cat isn't real. You know that.'

'She says you made Daddy go away.'

Laura rolled to a stop and sat, breathing. Aoife sucked on her cuddly minion's leg. Laura pictured this creature called Cat from a patchwork of crayon drawings on the fridge, slowly winking a snakey eye.

'And what else does Cat say about me?'

'Um... She says you're trying to poison me.'

'Oh, really? Well, you can tell her to cut the crap.'

'She says that you want to get rid of me.'

'You can tell her to shut her goddamn mouth, OK?'

'She says that you don't love me because there's something wrong with me...'

'You can tell Cat that I love you more than anything and she can't take you away from me, no matter what she does.'

Laura stared at the pretty house next to the car, one of a row of pretty houses with clipped shrubbery, like some fucking stupid biscuit box picture. The idea of normal was everywhere and it was this completely impossible thing. Without warning, a sob grabbed her by the throat and left her heaving, actually wailing through both hands covering her face. Aoife started crying too, in that weird dry way kids sometimes did. Laura caught her eye through her fingers in the rear-view mirror. OK then, she thought.

'I did make Daddy go away.' She wiped her nose on her sleeve.

'Wh—h-hyyy?' Aoife moaned, clutching the toy to her chest. She was so like a normal kid in this moment that Laura teared up again for a completely different reason. She turned around, filled with compassion for this little being who wasn't a Satan child after all.

'I hurt Daddy's feelings very badly. I broke a promise.'

'That's what Cat said you did.'

'But I'm very sorry about it.'

'Why did you break your promise?'

'Because I was sad, baby.'

Laura started the car back up. Aoife sat subdued, sucking on the leg again. How simple they were sometimes. A basic explanation was enough to suffice for all the incomprehensible crap of life.

Having left the town, they were now entering the dark stretch of fir plantation that covered the distance until the next town.

'Hey, Mummy, do you think this forest is enchanted?' It was less a forest and more like one big hedge, all the trees planted in precise straight lines. But Aoife's voice was full of glee, her sadness immediately forgotten.

'Well, it looks pretty dark in there, doesn't it? Yeah, I'd say it probably was.' Aoife stared at the places where the branches crossed, probably glimpsing all manner of fantastical things.

'You know what, Mummy?'

'What?'

'I bet that's where Cat came from.'

'Yeah, I bet.'

'So you do believe me that she's real!' Laura looked at her bright little daughter. The enchanted forest rolled by, reflected in her eyes.

'She's real inside your head, baby.'

'Just like I'm real inside of yours?'

'Um, yeah.'

And they drove on.

The shortest route on the map is not the quickest

from the anthology I am because You are

Pippa Goldschmidt

He wanted to meet in some café behind Waterloo station. I hadn't heard of it before and it wasn't on the internet. But clearly the cabbies liked it because the narrow street outside was full of their taxis all parked up in neat rows – like black metal beetles waiting to carry out an insect invasion of London.

We got our coffees and I started by asking him about his time in Helmand. This confused him, how relevant was it to the real problem? But you have to approach these things crabwise, sidling up.

Anyway, it didn't take too long before he started to talk. He told me about travelling the roads in slow convoys at a precise speed, all the tanks bunched together so that nobody would get left behind. About knowing you were being watched by the enemy hunkered down just beyond the horizon and not being able to do anything about it. About seeing the road ahead all kinked through a periscope. About scanning, constantly scanning every track and inch for things that shouldn't be there.

When I considered that the time was right, I led him back from that distant place. I asked him how long he'd taken to pass the Knowledge.

'Two and a half years,' and his voice plumped up with pride. Fair enough. Most people who attempt it, if they pass it at all, take far longer than that.

'Tell me, is there a special map that you cabbies use?'

He shook his head, 'Maps are almost useless. You start with the end-points of each route that you have to know, say Manor House Tube to Gibson Square. That's the very first one you learn. But what if one of the streets is blocked with roadworks or an accident, or just buggered up with traffic? So you need to learn alternative routes. And the best way to do that is to go there and experience it. One foot in front of the other. Slow and steady.'

I couldn't hide my astonishment, 'You walked all the routes in the Knowledge? But aren't there more than three hundred of them?'

He nodded. 'Well, the weather's a bit better here than in Helmand. And the walking's safer.' Then he ducked his head, 'Actually I cycled a few of the longer ones. Call me a cheat if you want.' And he grinned, so a certain shy charm that must have spent its time hidden away inside him could now be spotted breaking through the surface.

He positioned two fingers some way apart on either side of his cup. 'When you do the Knowledge you've got to learn how to negotiate around that coffee. It's large, it's hot and it's causing a hell of a traffic problem.'

I watched as he traced some imaginary routes on the formica table top. Some were graceful arcs, others irritable little detours that travelled straight up to the cup and then buckled around it at the last minute.

'The sooner you're warned about the coffee, the better state you're in. The more possibilites you have and the quicker the detour will be.' He smiled. He looked like he'd solved a major problem and perhaps he had. 'City's a creature in time as well as space. A traffic jam starts on one road, soon it'll shit on the whole area. There's feedback in the system. Walking, you get to learn the correct timescales for things to pass, for everything to normalise.'

'What about GPS?' I asked.

'What about it?' and he laughed. 'It'll just send you down an alley full of dustbins or stick you behind a million buses on Piccadilly.'

The second meeting. I'd read up beforehand, about mine clearance in Helmand. What he'd told me seemed unlikely but not impossible, and I found myself looking at manhole covers in a rather different way. I was beginning to see the space between what he told me and who he was. In cases like this it was always essential to find it because if all I had to go on were his words, things would be difficult for both of us.

'I like to work at night,' he said straight off, after we'd been served our coffees.

This was the first time he'd admitted to any feelings so I made a note of it.

'In the city the sky's the same colour as rusty old cars.' This reminded him of something, 'You got a lot of abandoned vehicles on the roads and quite often they were booby-trapped.'

He was sipping his coffee rather delicately I thought. It was easy to imagine his hands supporting the weight of a gun, fingers curved around its trigger. But I had to be careful with imagination, it had misdirected me in the past.

'You want darkness in the city at night – you look at the buildings, not the sky. Rows of black windows so regular they must be telling you a story,' and he drummed his fingers on the table.

'Of course a lot of the city just ignores the darkness. Shops, cafes, pubs – they all stay open. You've got to get out some distance if you want real night-time. Drive right out into the suburbs. There's a beautiful emptiness about a shuttered Tube station after midnight, with no-one around but dogs picking at rubbish and eyeing you up like you're an intruder on their territory. And perhaps you are. Sometimes I go out there and turn off the engine, just to sit and watch for the moment each morning when you see the land separate itself from the sky and drop back down. Then I go back home.'

'Where's your home?'

'Near Manor House tube.'

The starting point of the Knowledge's first route. Very neat. Maybe too neat. Maybe

I was being led somewhere, deliberately.

'And you lived there with – ' I left the question open for him, but he just sat there seemingly lost in the remains of the afternoon, with the café emptying out all around us and the proprietor stacking crockery in a noisy manner on the long metal counter. When finally he did speak, it took me by surprise.

First he tilted his cup so it could capture the sunlight and the white china gleamed at us both. Then he told me about her. 'She worked at the university. She took me there once, and I was surprised at how small the entrance to her department was. How a place that dealt with such big questions could be tucked away like it didn't care if anyone even noticed it or not. Her office wasn't much more a cupboard and piled high with stacks of paper. So much paper in there she could hardly see out of the window. Made me wonder just how much had been written down and recorded in there.' He moved the cup around while he talked. By now it was right on the edge of the table and the proprietor was hovering nearby, wanting us to pay.

On the way home I wondered about his night-time dogs picking at rubbish. When have you seen dogs doing that in the suburbs of London?

The third meeting took place the next day. Again, it was quite late in the afternoon.

'The land is revealed by the light most clearly in the morning or evening, when the Sun's right low down. Then you see all the bumps and hollows of the shadows. Noon is no good for anything. No information in the midday Sun.'

He was talking like there hadn't been a break, like he hadn't spent the previous night criss-crossing the streets of the city, driving people to where they needed to be. It was a gift he had, I could tell, to pick up where he left off. Like we were always in the present moment together.

I wondered if he was the sort of cabbie who enjoyed talking to his fares.

'Not usually, I can oblige them if they expect it but I don't initiate. Although more and more tourists nowadays want the patter from us. It's a persona. But that's ok because it's nothing really to do with me. Leaves my mind free to wander.'

The Sun was shining fierce through the café windows and the only shadow was cast by the streetlight outside, slanting a thick and dark line right across the table. He positioned his little espresso cup in this shadow.

'What did she do?' I asked.

'Dark matter,' and we both almost laughed at the absurdity of it, of sitting there in a café with squeezy plastic tomatoes of ketchup on each table, talking about something called dark matter.

'When we first met,' he said to me, 'she used to talk quite a lot about her work. She was trying to map some invisible stuff out there,' and he waved his hand at the grey London sky, 'stuff that wasn't lit up with stars like a Christmas tree. Her words for it, not mine. In return I told her about the city. And a bit about the land too. What I'd seen and not seen.'

The Sun had disappeared some time ago behind the clouds and the cup was left sitting in the flat grey light of the afternoon.

'The land?'

'Here and there. Now and then.' It was then that he first told me about the bundle of rags he'd glimpsed in the distance through the periscope of the tank. The bundle of rags that was lying heaped in the middle of the road so that you could easily imagine it was wrapped around a body. It looked to him about the size of a small child or a large animal.

Don't stop to see what it is, they'd been commanded, and so they hadn't. The convoy had kept going at the same precise speed as it approached the bundle, neither slowing down nor speeding up. You could get used to travelling that way, he told me, it felt like you were moving through space, just floating along. Until you looked through the periscope and reminded yourself what was all around you.

Don't even swerve to avoid it, they'd been commanded. So they'd had to run right over the top of it, feeling the tank shudder like it was breathing as it did so. And the rest of the convoy had done the exact same thing. It could have been a booby trap, designed to lure them out, or make them change track onto the mines. Or it could have been exactly what it appeared, an abandoned body. How were they supposed to know?

'I told her all about it. I wanted someone else to be able to picture it. The rest of the convoy never spoke of it. I checked the underside of the tank afterwards, picked out a piece of rag.'

We sat in silence. The shadow had returned to the table, which was a relief, it gave me something to concentrate on. I wanted to ask him more, but what could he tell me? I had to return to London and his girl.

'How long were you and her – '

About a year or so, he reckoned. A year of being happy together. He was happy, at any rate.

'How did you meet?'

She was a fare, of course. He picked her up at Victoria station and she asked him to take her to her office, and then started arguing with him about whether he was really going the quickest route. She told him to go straight along Exhibition Road and then Cromwell. He was used to this argument, even as he drove her left-right, left-right through the choppy little mews streets of Knightsbridge, ignoring what she was saying.

It could have ended there, with both of them feeling a little bit annoyed and no tip for him. But she spilt a load of papers over the seat and floor, and was still scrabbling to gather them up by the end of the journey. So he parked the cab, turned the meter off, and told her she had all the time in the world. She thanked him. He was only being polite but then they happened to glance at each other in the rear view mirror.

'Sometimes, looking at another human in a mirror is better than face to face,' he told me. 'You notice more.' He made some gesture with his hand that I couldn't follow. And I didn't understand why she'd told him to drive that route, because it wasn't the right way at all from Victoria station. Perhaps she'd got the names of the streets wrong.

Anyway, they'd had this year together. And he'd been shown some photographs of long, thin curves of light in the dark sky. Nothing at all like normal stars, this light was all stretched out and bent. She'd seemed proud of those photos. It was only in this distorted light pattern, she told him, that you could discover the truth about the dark matter, the stuff that did the distorting, wrapping space and time up into knots. They were in bed when she told him this.

I cleared my throat, slightly embarrassed, and made a note of all this in my little book. We drank the rest of our coffee in silence. I didn't say anything because I wanted to hear him talk some more.

The proprietor took our cups away and then in a deliberate manner also removed the napkins, the teaspoons, the wipe-clean menus, the sugar bowl, the salt and pepper shakers and finally the plastic tomato. There was nothing on the table now. He had to speak.

He spoke. A year later, and almost exactly to the day after they first met, she left him. There hadn't been any warning about it, she just disappeared into thin air. She'd always kept her own flat, and so for a couple of days he assumed she was there. They didn't live in each other's pockets, he didn't own her. He said this quite vehemently as if I'd been arguing this point with him. She was her own woman.

'Did you ask at the university?'

He nodded, of course. But they wouldn't tell him anything. He'd only been to one departmental party with her so nobody really knew him there.

Finally he'd gone round to her flat. And that was when things had really turned upside down, because another man had answered the door. Had leant against the door frame, wearing nothing but a dressing gown and smoking a cigarette, listening to his frantic questions. Had said through the smoke that he didn't know anything about her. Had never even heard of her. Could have been lies, could have been the truth. How could he tell?

He'd hung around the flat for a bit, not doing anything, just watching but someone must have noticed because the police arrived. He couldn't afford to get into any trouble. If he did, he'd lose his blue badge and his livelihood.

There was a tiny trail of sugar crystals leading across the table that I hadn't noticed before. I wrote down the address of this flat, it was the obvious place to start. 'What colour dressing gown?' I asked.

He didn't seem surprised at this. 'Brown.' He indicated his cup, 'Coffee-coloured, I guess. Espresso.'

He'd tried asking at the places where they used to go together, the pubs and restaurants and so on. But of course nobody could tell him anything. And now he didn't know what else to do.

'So I just thought that all I could do was look around. But where to start?'

It was then that he realised. Maybe the best thing to do would be to simply let his fares decide for him. Every route would take him somewhere different and he could keep his eyes open, scanning the landscape for her. She had to be out there, somewhere. On the street, sitting in a café, hidden in a building. She was still in the city, he was sure of it. He even felt he must have looked at her during his searches, without realising exactly where she was. Without being able to see her directly.

I shut my notebook. 'I'll agree there's a logic to your method,' I told him, 'but it is pretty random.'

He nodded and almost smiled. That was the whole point. He'd tried the other approach, but the quickest way of working through the entire city was to travel randomly, and let other people decide for you where you should go. Of course the fares didn't know that when he was driving them to their destinations he was searching, searching all the time. They didn't know what an essential function they had in his life. And maybe hers.

'So why do you want me to look as well?' I asked him. 'If this is the perfect method, then what can I add to it?'

'I'm not sure,' he said. 'But I can't stop working, because when I'm working I'm looking for her. And if I do stop working I'm still thinking about her and me, and how it was between us. I'm just very tired and I thought that you're a neutral person, you've got no connection with either of us. You may be able to see the pattern in all this that I can't. There's always a pattern, isn't there?'

I thought it was time to make some things clear to him, 'The thing is, I look for people who don't want to be found. That's the biggest pattern. They have a reason, even if you don't know what it is at first. But when you work it out, you're halfway there to finding her.' I even told him a little bit about a recent case, the Butter Boy case, because it had involved me travelling through a collection of small villages that weren't obviously linked by anything more than the randomness of geography, and a network of dilapidated roads now superseded by a nearby motorway. I felt it might be similar to this case. Butter Boy had had his reasons, that was for sure. Reasons I grew to understand and respect, and that was why I'd declined to collect my fee from his frantic wife, in the end all her lies becoming as clear as a code that I'd learnt how to crack.

Eventually I fell silent and we sat and listened to the rhythmic swish as the proprietor swept the floor, working his broom around each of the chair legs in turn.

When he'd first told me about the dark matter I'd thought it even more unlikely than his experiences in Helmand. Perhaps I'd doubted too much in my life. But it seemed to be real or at least, a lot of people had convinced themselves it was real without actually seeing it, which wasn't the same thing at all but would have to do for now.

'Tell me honestly,' I said. 'What exactly was in those photographs she showed you?'

He looked away. Right down at the floor and beyond, as if he were really looking at something a long way beneath it. Behind me I could hear the proprietor pause.

A Siege Inverted

Henry King

'An extra seventy pounds a month,'
the agent said, to see the city
walls outside our kitchen window;

that would be almost another tenth!'
– she tells me, as we walk below
this crenelated stonework, once

constructed for the town's defence;
only patrolled now, if at all,
by tourists and local residents.

Us the most recent. Weeks before,
I slept in rooms where another wall
– of concrete, covered in graffiti –

was visible. Although we saw
no soldiers on patrol, no sentries,
we knew they were there anyway

but not for our protection. Today
I walk with bags from Morrison's
back to my house (for which the rent

is seventy less per month) past stones
that have outlasted sieges, centuries,
even the people they were meant

to keep safe, and to keep at bay.

Bethlehem – York, July 2012

Not Climbing Mount Sion
for Gabriel Levin

Henry King

Once I'd got halfway up the western slope
of the Kidron Valley, taking a dirt path
that led directly up the hillside – the gradient
must've been nearly forty-five degrees –
the loose earth underfoot began to slip,
and I had to grab handfuls of earth to stop
myself from falling. Lowell's 'You never climbed
Mount Sion' kept on coming to mind,
although I knew this wasn't the right hill;
but Zion Gate was just a short way south
if I could only make it to the top...

Ram's-horn trumpets blew from the cemetery
behind me: Orthodox Jews among the radiant
sunset-lit stone, making a cacophony
that said all anybody could about grief.
Last Easter at my grandmother's funeral
I stood and read out over her coffin, 'I will
lift up mine eyes unto the hills, from whence
cometh my help?' Now, it was a relief
to reach the road and clamber over the wall,
with no breath left for a Song of the Ascents
– just curses, gasps for air, and blasphemies.

The Paddock-Stuil Stew

Jason Henderson

Mangst oor man-makkit maginks
Thare ur shuirly few
As richt frichtsom as
The paddock-stuil stew.

Yon caddie o daith
Kin lave fowk mankit by its spew,
Left mair than jist dumfounnert
By the paddock-stuil stew.

If its merls o doome flee
Goam apocalypse noo,
An yit thay maun invest
In the paddock-stuil stew.

The bastardin deil
Wae a wide, wicket smue:
Winze o the warld
Is the paddock-stuil stew.

But it's a stane o distructioun
That wull nivir be threw,
Still an on ye're telt it's needit:
The paddock-stuil stew.

Thay'll anoonce it's a deterrent
An thay'll whid an thay'll skew,
Jist tae dimit aw the protests
Agin the paddock-stuil stew.

Sic a tadger meisurin gemme
Shuid mak ye greet an grue,
As thay fecht tae huv the lairgeſt
Paddock-ſtuil ſtew.

Thoosans hungert an in puirtith
Is naethin new,
Sae thay'll crack oan wae the ſpendin
Fir the paddock-ſtuil ſtew.

Care na by fur the bairns
Wae puggies faur fae fu –
We huv tae affuird
The paddock-ſtuil ſtew.

Sae whan weans ur eatin fae fid-banks
Hou kin it ſtull be yer view
Tae pish awa aw that siller
Oan the paddock-ſtuil ſtew?

Rehearsals for the End of Time

Ron Butlin

Leuchars railway station, on the line between Edinburgh and Dundee, is a place where
time often seems to have stopped. Forever.

Room heaters switched off, and all lights.
Doors locked, steel shutters pulled down,
benches removed. Arctic winds and
North Sea sleet scour every surface
of its history.

No pyramids, no Renaissance,
no rise and fall of mighty empires –
not now. Not ever.
Only this battened-down brickwork. Only me
going nowhere.

I'm sure it was a summer's day when I came across
the metal footbridge. I remember sunlight.
Mid-January now by the feel of it,
and the clock's hands stuck
at a quarter-past ten . . .

(Once upon a time I lived in the warm hills
above Barcelona,
I'd stroll each evening beneath shower upon
shower of falling stars. So many wishes to make,
so many lifetimes to look forward to . . .)

These are Scottish stars hammered
into East Coast darkness,
right up to the hilt.
Bringing the Cosmic Wheel to a standstill.

An RAF jet hangs silent and motionless 100ft or so
above platform 2 –
had it been planning to liberate someone,
somewhere? Was it en route to yet another country
to help them become
just like us?

No train in sight, nor hope of any.

Rehearsals for the End of Time
take place, it seems,
here at Leuchars station

Tripping

Alan Harkness

mountain bound

        sun on the back

faltering ascent

        up by the burn

each uisge eas fors

cold expanse

always stars

tramping fire

each uisge eas fors

empty mountain

        journey on

Life's a Goat

Joan Lennon

sketch the line
horizontal across the cliff face –

momentum describes
the route –

stratigraphy felt
rather than observed –

there's precious little room
for mapping

or the smell of rain
on rock

or the semi-circularity
of vistas –

the brief distraction of a
feather on the wind

and gravity ensues

The Welsh Medievalist

Sally Evans

The Welsh Medievalist
The cuckoo calls *cu-yu,* where is she?
Warblers and robins nest silent
while doves sing an alto – *whisht, whisht.*

The Welsh medievalist hears
across woods, across centuries,
cu-yu, cu-yu. Deserted.

A poet we cannot know
in a book we cannot find – where is it?
Here it is – *cu-yu, cu-yu.*

In the isles of the sea,
lost to us, impostor,
tempting from the branches,

cu-yu, cu-yu,
birdsong's language
behind our tongues

as we listen, wish an answer
through the coverts, *cu-yu,*
where is she, where is she?

We strain for echoes
of long-loved languages
and those who spoke them

when the wicked bird – *cu-yu*
comes in May to display
Spring's loss of all past.

Yon hill ye descendit last year wi the weans

Ross McGregor

Yon hill ye descendit last year wi the weans
Will ay be a marker for wur faimily's pains
The doonhill tummle ae junk an life-forms
An the hut made ae wid an moss an worms
The beauty ae rustit undulatin fire
The vomit an rest an the guilt ae clipped heather
Pinned tae yer jaiket for the appreciation ae owls' een
Watchin ye dance a' nicht wi rubber blue-soled shuin

September 2014

Peter Burnett

They called it discussion, sometimes debate,
But the drumming sound was folk defending their conclusions
All day until the deadline date.

Tyrants emerged, preached to their own,
New to the game I would forgive them that,
But anger surged as the same ideas went bowlin' roon.

It was like the schoolyard banter I played part of as a child
Except that each day the drummers retreated to their corners, none the wiser,
And when it was over — hegemony lit a cigarette, and smiled.

Extract from the novel *The Wolf Trial*

Neil Mackay

Chapter Sixteen

The Committee for Public Inquiry is convened, and I begin my dialogues with the Werewolf, and learn of his practises in the woods and by night

Paulus convened a Committee of Public Inquiry – on the spot, standing in the dust of the town square. He dragged me aside – truly dragged me, by hand, and quite fierce – and screamed for Karfreitag like he was screaming for a medicine to quell pain. The sergeant ran up to us at a trot.

'You,' Paulus said, pushing me in the chest, 'are to get Rodinan – he is the one head man I have not seen. Take the boy Raban. Get to his house and bring him here.'

Paulus said he intended to prepare indictments for murder against anyone knowingly involved in releasing the child into the woods, if it could be proved they did so with the intention of the boy being used as bait to catch the werewolf. Indictments were also laid against those who killed the Stumpf sons. Paulus said full power of deputy was invested in me and I should use it. If I failed to use it, I would be judged unfit for service. Paulus had never spoken to me in such a way before, and it scared me as I was not well trained in interrogation, despite having watched Paulus at his work. I stood a little dumb as I listened to him.

Paulus pushed me again. 'Go,' he shouted. I ran to Raben, and heard Paulus tell Karfreitag, 'Get that bastard Jens here on the double. And tell your soldiers to keep near Kroll and Odil – I do not want them talking to each other without our ears close by.'

The councillor Rodinan lived far out by the forest. The house sat in a cleared woodland patch and was built big, strong and square – two stories high, white-washed and with a long porch running around all four sides, the door set below a Greek style Doric arch. Very artistic in its design. A wooden love seat was coddled in a thicket of red and yellow rose bushes.

Raben said to me that he thought it best if he waited away from the house and did not come with me to the door when we made the head of the path to the Rodinan home. 'It would offend him and make your job more difficult,' he said. I agreed and walked on to the house.

'Hello,' I called, for the house seemed abandoned and cold. 'Is anyone home?'

I heard laughter from the back of the house, and walked around the white panelled side wall. There was a sharp bark, the bark of a little dog, and more laughter – light and crackling, the laugh of a child.

Behind, the house, there was a small kitchen garden, and a patch of grass. A boy of maybe ten sat upon a barrel by the back wall and watched a little girl – she could have been no more than six – kneeling on all fours on the ground. A dog – a badger hound – was clambering on her back. The girl's dress was rucked up on her hips, and she was bare beneath. The girl laughed and the dog thrust at her – pink and pointed and wet – and barked. The boy did not move or speak or take his eyes off the girl and the dog.

I stood for a moment, confounded. The boy, I realised, I had seen before – it was Rodinan's son, one of the children I had watched frogging. Filus. The girl I had not seen – the child in front of me was young, and the sister I had met was older than the boy Filus.

'Stop,' I shouted, and the boy sprang up like a jangling puppet. The little girl laughed and rolled onto her back, the dog licked her belly. She scratched its head and laughed more and wrestled in play with the dog on the grass. It sat on her cross-wise, still hard and hammering its hips. The dog looked back at me.

I crossed the yard and kicked the dog in the ribs. It rode across the grass like a kickball, and lay there in a hedgerow yampering and crying out. It could not stand or take a breath, and I brought my foot down on its head. The children were screaming and a woman came out of the house, through a back kitchen door, along with a girl – the older sister I had met before at frogging. The woman screamed, 'Martin.'

I shouted at her, 'What is going on here? Are these your children?'

She ran back into the house, crying, 'Martin, Martin. Come quick.'

A man emerged – it was Rodinan, and he hefted a short sword in his hand. I raised my palms in peace and said, 'Sir.'

He recognised me, and looked to the dog and his children and said, 'What have you done?' He pushed his oldest daughter back into the house behind him. She squealed and ran into the dark corridor.

'I came upon your children, sir,' I said. 'The dog was attacking the young girl in a way I cannot think to speak of and your son was doing nothing. I killed the animal.'

The little girl was wrapped around her mother's skirts and screamed – like a Devil, 'Bjorn was playing with me. You hurt him. You are bad.'

'Sir,' I said, and looked at Rodinan's wife for shame and then looked down, 'the dog was on your daughter's back. It was trying to couple with her.'

Rodinan looked at his son and said, 'Filus?'

'Bjorn was getting rough just as this gentleman appeared, father. Eloise was not scared though. I did not think anything was wrong. They were playing rough and tumble.'

'Son,' I said, 'that dog was going to hurt your sister.'

I spoke to the mother and father now, 'Please, I am sorry if I have upset your family, but I feared for what was going to happen. Your children, it seemed, did not understand what they were seeing.'

'They are innocent,' said the mother, fierce at me. 'Did you have to kill it?'

'I am sorry,' I said.

The little girl ran to the dog in the corner of the garden and lay over it. 'Bjorn, Bjorn,' she said and she cried.

'I am sorry,' I said.

Her mother went to fetch her, the girl's dress and hands were thick with mud and covered in blood now. The boy began to cry and walked to his mother. She held him, and the girl let her mother go and walked past me to her father, casting me a tear-stained scowl.

Rodinan told the girl, 'Get out of those filthy clothes, Eloise, and go to the pump and wash. You are dirty.'

The child stopped still and stripped naked on the grass, standing between me and her father. She slipped off her dress like a snake shucking skin, then stepped lightly, with high pointing toes, as if she half-danced, to her father's side.

'But father,' she said. 'It will be cold.' She curled her leg around his leg and slid her arm between his thighs – ivy on a tree.

He knelt and kissed her on the mouth and said, 'Once you have the worst of this filth off you, I will pour a hot bath in the kitchen for you, and wash you. Does that make you happy?'

'Yes, father,' she said, and she ran skipping to the pump. The pump was down near where the dog lay, and she did not cast the animal a second glance as she stepped over it, took the pump handle and put her head beneath the gush. She squealed and laughed and stamped as the cold water fell over her.

Rodinan threw his sword at the ground and it stuck in the grass, juddering. 'What was it you came to see me about, young man?' he asked. 'Or did you just come to kill my daughter's dog?'

'Bjorn was my dog too, father,' said the boy.

'Get in the house,' Rodinan said, and his face fell cold with anger. He took the boy by the neck and pulled him from his mother's waist.

'You are a failure. You should protect your sister,' he said, and threw the boy into the house through the back kitchen door into the dark corridor. 'Get out of my sight.'

His wife, picked up her skirts and walked quickly through the door behind her son.

'Please bring us some wine,' Rodinan said, as she passed him. 'It is a pleasant day and we can take our talk outside.'

His wife nodded.

'I have some seats at the front of our house. Sit with me there and tell me what your master wants. I take it you come on his orders?'

'Yes, sir,' I said. 'I come with his full authority, which means the authority of the state and the Prince-Bishop. I will not need wine, but you may take some if you wish.'

He turned his head on his neck to look at me, as if it would break.

I gestured before me, and said, 'The seats you spoke of, sir. Shall we go there?'

He walked stiff around the side of his house and I followed him. His back and shoulders were tensed and hard, and scared, I knew. After we talked, I took him with me, and he drank no wine. Raben and I escorted him to the town.

* * * * *

When we returned, Paulus had commandeered the main hall for the Committee of Public Inquiry, and instructed Fromme's boy to draw up a list of witnesses for the first round of interviews with townsfolk. There would be a running order to decide who would be called to give solemn evidence before criminal law in the case of the child who had vanished from the keep.

'I could have done this job, sir,' I said.

'No,' said Paulus, and he grabbed me by my collar and dragged me behind him. 'I have need of you.'

He shouted over his shoulder at Raben, 'Keep councillor Rodinan by you, please constable.'

'Am I to stay here?' Rodinan shouted back.

'You are.' And Paulus draggged me on behind him like a puppy on a string.

I was tired of this man-handling and wrested myself out of his grasp. 'Let me go, god damn you, sir,' I said. 'I am not a dog – and you have not treated me as such, so do not treat me now.'

He stopped, and a look of outrage passed over his face – it vanished, like a wind blew it away – and he nodded. And then he bowed – which took me off me guard. 'Of course,' he said. 'I am busy, and things are urgent. I need you, and was unthinking. Apologies.'

'Of course,' I said, and I bowed back, but he was already off on his way again and missed my graciousness. I ran behind him. He made for the keep.

'Hurry up,' he shouted.

When we arrived at the black iron and wood door of the keep he told me, 'Say nothing to him about the death of his sons.'

The keep was a windowless four-tier cake – and Paulus had examined it well, many times, for he felt it was his property, and I had tagged along behind once or twice as I was interested in the construction of buildings and how they were made for purpose: why a kitchen is better there, say, than a store-room here or quarters. We had studied such issues in a mathematics class on architecture and it was one of the few topics under examination in that subject which I took to with an interest, and performed well at when tested. The first layer of the keep was below ground. The cells and the armoury – and it made sense to me to station these important parts of the building subterranean. Two rooms were set aside for holding prisoners. One, large, and big enough to hold a single prisoner and to conduct an interrogation. It also held the instruments of interrogations – this was where Stumpf was kept. The second room was of the same proportions – just a fraction smaller, perhaps – with a long cage inside to hold a group of prisoners. A fair way to divide and organise the custodial side of the keep's work, I reckoned. Between the cells and the armoury there were many passages, with bricked up or empty rooms on every side. This was an unholy waste of space, I thought. The rooms could have been employed for storage of some sort, I imagined. The armoury was small – a room split in two, with weapons lined on the walls, and barrel upon barrel of gunpowder and explosives locked inside a cage which ran from floor to ceiling at the rear. In the floor of the corridor outside the armoury, there was a hatch which led down to an old bolt-run that led under the walls of the keep, ten feet or more below the earth, and came out in the ground behind the walls, hard up against the mountain – a tunnel and route to escape if enemy came in through the iron-bound front door. Sensible and not unexpected, in my opinion – all defensive quarters need a method of retreat, otherwise siege is the only recourse when outnumbered or outgunned. Above, on the first floor there was the congregation room, the wash rooms, the kitchens, offices for Jens and the quarter-master, and a mess-hall. This seemed ergonomic and wise in its partitioning and design. Next, on the second storey were the quarters. I would have placed quarters here as well – again, it was ergonomic. Though, perhaps, the armoury might have best placed on this level too – near to the sleeping guards. On the third floor, the provisions were kept – wine, beer, dried fruit, pickled vegetables, flour, salted meat. Enough for months. I thought this positioning a mistake – and would have hived off part of the ground floor for provision, to keep food nearer the kitchens and mess-hall, and prevent the expending of unnecessary energy by the guards up and down the stairs. The fourth floor was the open roof – crested with battlements shoulder high. A stairway and hatch led up and the men often practised their combat up there in the clear air, we were told. I liked this feature, it added a dash of theatre to an otherwise municipal and unoriginal building – despite its black and lour air. In all, I would have given the keep's architect a mark of six out of ten.

Paulus and I walked in through the heavy wood and iron-bound front door – four men wide, two men high, as thick as a human body, of excellent defensive design. We made our way down to the cells in the orange torch light.

Down there, Stumpf said he knew nothing of the boy – until he found him in the woods at night. He did not know the child was even the son of the man and woman he had killed that afternoon. He knew a child had fled, but he had not seen its face.

Paulus talked to our wolf, Peter, but the wolf did not answer beyond a yes or a no. The wolf was respectful but the wolf did not like Paulus – though he looked at me, while the three of us sat there – him in his double cage, us without.

'Willie?' Paulus said to me.

'Sir?'

'I do not think Master Stumpf wishes to speak to me.'

Time stopped for a handful of seconds and I thought to myself – this is the moment, Willie, when you can make your name. I was not afraid, and I did not doubt myself. Unlock this man Stumpf before you, I thought, and you will unlock a world of fortune and fame for yourself.

'I am happy to take over if you wish a rest, sir,' I said.

Stumpf – burned and bloody and a little broken – looked pleased with himself. Paulus seemed shamed that he had not made his prisoner talk, but he was not a man for the whip at the first turn of events. He wanted Stumpf's story, and did not mind how we got it – so he left the cell.

I poured us both beer from a clay jug, and passed Stumpf his cup through the double cages. I raised my cup to him. We drank, and I waited a little while.

'What was it like to kill that boy?' I asked.

'Easy,' said Stumpf.

'I would like to hear about it,' I said.

'Why?' Stumpf asked.

'Because it fascinates me,' I replied.

Stumpf giggled to himself, a chirruping laugh, like a wicked bird – a strange note in the throat of a man so big and worldly and bright.

'Of course I knew the boy in the woods that night. I saw him that afternoon with his parents, and I saw him run,' he said, 'but I was dealing with his father, while his mother still lived, and could not get to him. He was gone. Later, once all was done, I looked for him. But from far – in the trees – I saw he was with the women at their washing. Greet was there, by hell. Our own Greet. Come the night, I was in the woods, and there he was. I ate him.

The boy, and the sixty some that I killed – that you talk to me about – I was not in uniform when I killed them. And this I want you to know – I killed many more back when I was wearing a military badge.

Have you ever felt the need to put your hand in fire – so great that you did it? Or to jump from a cliff? Steal something you did not need? I can recount all of them for you it you want – give you enough to fill up your little notebook twice over with detail. However, they were all the same, but they were all different as well.

I skinned a man once – back when I was in uniform. And that does not count. On the orders of my commander. A year before the siege of Munster, perhaps. I removed the pink skin gloves from his hands, shaved off his sleeves, the skin from his legs, stripped his back and belly like I was removing the coat from a gentleman. He was so red and quivering – just bare, by a fraction, to the world. I peeled off his face – slit from hairline to ear, round the jaw, slashes at the eyes, nose and mouth – and if you pull, the face, it slides away. I unmanned him as well. My skinning skills were not fit to do that bit better and leave him there, between his legs, still in tact but peeled and dangling raw.

Naked man. It was the wrong man, though. It was his brother we wanted. We never caught the brother. I was decorated – given another war ribbon for my good service.

But the ones that I killed in my woodsman's clothes – the ones you say count – I can recount them if you want – all for you, as I said. Though it would be better if you just let me tell you about my best.

In each act, I sought certain elements. Moments, sensations, reactions – roles that I could play and which they could play. I have always loved plays, drama – especially the old miracle plays. Modern plays – of princes that reign over us and the like – or history plays with Caesar and Alexander – I can read about those people and events in books, so on the stage they do not interest me. I like make-believe. It's been a long time, however, since I have seen actors perform upon the stage. So, I will tell you the story about my best one.

Most often, I would scout the roads around Bideburg – to see travellers coming to town. Everything has its rhythm, so if it was a lone traveller – and that is always a man – and I knew they could not reach the town by nightfall, then I'd shadow them through the woods and come the time they made camp – far out before the Dark Hedges – I'd wait for them to sleep and then it was done. A good event, though, would be a couple or a family passing through town – going out the other side, past the keep, and under the Steipplinger arch, on into the forest. They'd draw up at the inn, water their horses, check their cart, eat, drink, wash – and by then I would be far out in front of them – off past the keep, under the arch, and into the forest. Waiting. A prime arrival would be a party of noon visitors. They'd rest for maybe four hours, then head off again before dusk – the man driving while the family slept. I'd tie my horse in the woods and wait, three hours trek in front of them – so it was night when we met.

I find it comical that the chase which ended my run – that brought me here – that it was the first time I broke my pattern, my plan. I saw that family last Friday, and it was daylight, and it was not in the order that it should have been, the rhythm was wrong, but they were like fire, or jumping off a cliff or stealing and I thought I could do it – maybe in a new way, for the first time in a long time. In daylight. But I was wrong, and the boy got away, and so now I am your guest and interlocutor – is that the correct word for what I am?

Back to this best time, though – this perfect event, Willie – it was a mother, baby and father. I had a routine, which I am sure you would like to know. Wolves don't talk, you see, and I do. I'd stand in the road – always at a different point, for luck and not for any other reason – and as they approached, I would wave to them – hands flapping and friendly, high above my head. Dressed in my best peasant clothes – not ostentatious, not wretched either. The clothes of a good working man. I'd ask, 'Could you let me ride with you a little way up the road to my house?'

And this family – they said, yes, as nearly every family riding a cart did – because it is unfriendly and suspicious to do otherwise.

As we rode, I talked to them at first – for a good long time. Questions of their health, and their destination, and their family and what brought them on the road. Most folk, they love to talk only of themselves, but after a while, once they have told all their little tales and watched you listen – for that is what makes them happy – they will feel the need to ask you a little of yourself too, for they have nothing else to talk of, and then I would talk of God, my wife and children, my hard work and humble farm, and my happiness.

We'd ride along, content and safe and close with each other now, and there would often be a little silence, while we all thought of what we had said to each other. Such moments could be warm and dear.

Then I told my story. I always told my story – and it always worked. 'Sir,' I would say to the man, 'sir, this may sound like the wildest of claims, but there is something I must tell you.'

The man would turn around to look at me – where I sat propped up on their baggage and sacks in the wagon bed – and say, 'Oh, yes.'

'Sir,' I'd say, 'many years ago, I was in this wood on my thirteenth birthday and a fairy – now please wait and listen, believe me – a fairy told me that I would find my fortune here. That a good woodsman, and a good boy, who had served God his whole life would be rewarded with treasure – that was hidden somewhere amongst all these trees.'

The woman would usually turn too now, and say, 'Indeed? Are you playing with us or is this true?'

I would swear to Jesus that I spoke the truth. 'The fairy,' I told them, 'the fairy said to me that if I could find one true Christian spirit on the road, then that would guarantee that I would find the treasure. Just one honest person who loved God and had done no wrong. If they searched with me then I would find the treasure, and was honour bound – on my life and by God – to share what I discovered with them. But I have been travelling this stretch of road for years and searched with hundreds of folk hundreds of times, and still found nothing because I have not found an honest soul.'

This family – like most – would say, 'Then let's dig. We are good God-fearing folk.'

I would always say, 'I can see that. Tonight will be the night.'

And I would tell them that the fairy said whatever treasure was waiting was one hundred paces from the road. And off we would go into the woods. Sometimes the man would say that he'd bring a shovel with him, to dig the treasure up, but I would tell him it was not necessary as the treasure was just waiting there – perhaps a chest of diamonds or a great bag of gold – sitting on the ground, not hidden beneath the earth.

Often, once we were one hundred paces into the forest, and it started, the events went out of my immediate control. I liked this though – the running and chasing and fighting in the woods, that had no plan or rhythm to it, just action. This one, though – the best one, that I am talking of – this one was like a dance perfected over years, patterned perfectly in every way.

We took a torch – the husband, the father, carried it, the mother with the baby at her side – and we walked one hundred paces into the wood. By a great tree, I stopped and said, 'Pass me the light, sir.' I knelt. I said I saw something among the ferns and brambles. I dropped to my knees, rooted on the forest floor. I said, 'My God. It is true, look here. You must be good Christians.'

I stood and cast the torch down a little, the man dipped to look. I grabbed him by the hair and thrust the torch up into his face, and kicked his legs from under him. His hair took fire. He fell, screaming, beating his head, his cuffs now catching fire. I pulled my knife and turned on the wife, holding her baby. She screamed and ran, into the forest, not toward the road. That was fine and well – and what I wanted. They never ran towards the road – for it is in the forest that people think they can hide. On the road, you are bare to my eyes.

The flames were out now, on the man's head. I kicked him in the face and he went out and down, and I stamped on his ribs, to be safe. They cracked a little like dry twigs under my foot. I took his shoes off and slit the tendons at his ankles. He woke, crying in pain, and I beat his head off the great tree till he was out again. I tied his hands behind him with some bailing twine I carried in my pocket. The cinch cut him at the wrists.

I turned to the forest and shouted, 'I am coming for you and your baby.' When you run in fear – and you'll know this just as well as I – when you run in fear all you can hear is your own breath, your own footsteps, and your heart and blood. You think your pursuer can hear you swallow. And fear makes you clumsy and loud. I could hear the woman – the girl, eighteen, I guess – stumbling through the trees, maybe another hundred paces further into the wood.

I took up the torch and walked after her – waving it before me, so she could see its flame coming for her. Then there was silence. She'd stopped running and was hidden somewhere. I walked, and every minute or so I shouted, 'I can smell you.' I could see where she'd ran through the trees and bushes – stamping the ground flat and breaking stalks and thin branches. Then her baby cried. And then there was silence. She'd covered the baby's mouth, I knew. I listened hard and could hear the softest mewling – a wail behind a hand. I followed the noise. It took me to a run of deep bushes – she was inside, the white of her dress through the black green mesh, lying on her belly, pulled back hard inside her hiding hole, her baby cupped to her. The baby sobbing behind her hand was almost too soft to hear now, but it was still there, to my ear.

I stood and panted hard. 'Where is that bitch?' I said. 'I will find her.' The baby still sobbed – so quiet though. The sound smothered then, like a pillow on a face. I waited by the bushes, scratching myself, growling. A quarter hour went by, maybe. The smothered sobbing grew fainter and quieter and at last it ended in the softest of sighs ever heard by two people – me and her. I waited another minute. The bush quivered and then shook like it had come to life, and the bush screamed, 'My baby, my baby.'

I leant down and pulled the mother out by the hair – her baby, suffocated-blue and dead, in her arms. I took her baby from her and held it by the leg. I dragged her back to her husband, the child swinging at my side. The man was dying. I sat the woman down before him, and said, 'If you love him you can kill him.' She looked at me, mad, a ghost – not a woman anymore, though her figure was fine and her face, if fear had not been on it, would have been appealing.

'Or you can watch me kill him,' I said. And then I lifted her child to my mouth and

I tasted it, sir – the sweet calve meat from the fat of its back. She screamed, and I swung the child by its arm – the whoosh of it, a white circle in the black air. 'Be quiet,' I said, 'or I will throw your baby into the dark.' She was quiet and I gave her the baby. She cradled it.

Should I carry on? I worry that my confession is too much. But if you wish, then I will.'

Stumpf waited. I nodded. Stumpf nodded back to me, and continued.

'Her husband nodded too, like us – he nodded to me and asked his wife to kill him then, and I sat down to watch. She held her child, still, and crooned over her husband, as he kissed and touched her, though he was very weak. She didn't look at me but she said she would kill her husband, and he brushed her face.

'Good,' I said, 'well if you wish to do that then enjoy each other one more time.'

Neither understood at first, but they followed when I took my knife and told her to undress and to undress her husband too. And then they did what I told them to do on the floor of the forest. A dying man cannot perform, though, it seemed, so I set their baby between them and said, 'Be a family.'

Shall I go on? If that is what you want then I am happy to do so.'

I said, 'Go on, Stumpf.' And I held his eye for he wanted me to break away, and look down from his face.

'I watched them on the ground – eye to eye – and let them be a while, quiet and untroubled together. The wife told the husband, 'It will all be well.'

I told her, 'You should not have said that. Kill him. Now.' She went back on her word then, and would not kill him. But when I took their baby and threw it in the air, playing catch in the torchlight, they both agreed to get it done. It took her ten minutes or more to choke the life out of him – for I'd told her to use her hands on him and look her husband in the eye, kiss him when he said goodbye to her.

Afterwards, she was not a woman anymore – so I played animal games with her. I made her play a snuffling pig, a mule for riding, a breeding mare, a clucking chicken and then a breeding mare again. I stood and let her kiss me where I pleased, and then I watered her – telling her I rebaptised her as a good Christian woman now she had found the treasure.

I could have played with her all night. She sang and danced for me. She sang songs she'd sung to her baby in its crib, as it lay on the forest floor, and she held her dead husband on the ground beside the child.

Later, after much of this exploration, I asked her what her name was, and she could not say. She asked to die instead. Asked me to kill her. I told her she could hang herself if she wished, for I had to go home to my wife and children. She lifted her torn dress from the ground and made a knotted loop in it for her neck. She climbed one of the great old trees to the first branch – higher than a man she went. And she tied one end of her dress to a bough, looped the choke around her neck and slipped from the tree like a silk unrolled.

I watched her, and she turned back into a woman – a person. She took a little while to die. I felt sorry for her.

Do you see what had happened? I had killed no-one. She had killed them all – her baby, her husband, herself. This was the best, Willie.'

Stumpf nodded and said, 'Do you want me to go on? With more?'

I said, 'No. I do not want you to go on. You should be dead, and I will help kill you.'

Stumpf made a sound – a laugh, a sigh, a moan – and said, 'Yes.'

Paulus had returned to the cell, and stood in the shadows, quiet for a long while, but now he coughed – with such feigned respect – and the thread between Stumpf and I seemed to dissolve in the air like spider dust.

'May I ask a question, please?' asked Paulus.

'Yes,' I said – like a knee reflex, as if my physician had hit me with his hammer – and Paulus stepped forward into the light.

'Thank you, Willie,' he said.

I could not say sorry, so I just said, 'Sir.'

'If Willie says yes,' said Stumpf. 'then yes, sir, ask a question.'

Paulus said to Stumpf, 'Do you not see others as people?'

'What is a person? What are people?' asked Stumpf.

'Me. You, surely Stumpf. You say you are not a wolf, so what are you?'

'I am one of you,' he said.

And I would have killed Stumpf, if I had not believed in the full process of the law, and that justice should be above me.

The Wolf Trial by Neil Mackay will be published by Freight Books in Spring 2016

Never Not Sending Missives

The Midnight Letterbox: Selected Correspondence 1950-2010
Edwin Morgan, (Editors).
James McGonigal and John Coyle

Carcanet, £19.99, 534 pp

Edwin Morgan was not only one of the greatest Scottish poets of the twentieth century; he was also among the most fastidious when it came to cultivating his archive for the benefit of future generations. It is remarkable that for a poet so modern – so enamoured of the *now* – Morgan always kept one eye on posterity, but it should not be surprising. After all, as his famous poem 'Archives' inversely testifies, a generation can only be measured by what it has preserved.

The Edwin Morgan archive is shared among several libraries in Scotland, with the present volume – the first collection of Morgan's letters but not, one hopes, the last – drawn from the University of Glasgow's portion. As editors James McGonigal and John Coyle concede, it is 'a selection of a selection of a selection'. Even so, it is an impressive volume, covering sixty of the poet's most active years. It is also a revealing and, at times, moving journey: from the prologue of the poet's 'second life' in the 1960s, his coming out and instatement as *makar* in the 1990s, to the slow decline of his health over the following decade. It is not only a valuable scholarly resource, but an illuminating portrait of a singular figure

and his extraordinary generation.

As the editors attest, Morgan was always a chameleonic figure – '[t]here is a mimic quality to his letters: while the voice is always his, it also bends to the frequencies of his correspondent' – and the book's 500-odd pages give plenty of scope to show the poet at his various 'frequencies'. Recurring topics include concrete poetry, especially with fellow concretists such as Ian Hamilton Finlay. Morgan also reacts to the limits of the Scottish Renaissance and modernist tradition even as he asserts its successes (especially aspects of Hugh MacDiarmid's work). Additionally, the letters chart the trials, tribulations and triumphs of publication, especially in the extensive missives to Michael Schmidt, his major publisher throughout his life and after. At times the level of detail may appeal to scholars more than to general readers, but as testament to both the brightness of Morgan's voice and McGonigal and Coyle's selection process, such detail is rarely a turgid affair. The editorial notes, which appear after each letter, are perfectly pitched: brief and informative, peppered with charming anecdotes and a touching pithiness befitting of its subject.

Morgan is at his most enjoyable and infectious when talking about the things he loves. By his own admission, these are 'love, music, science, a new time'. Despite this, Morgan initially speaks little of love – a measure, no doubt, of the difficulties faced by a closeted gay man in twentieth-century Scotland, 'a new time' or no. It is sheer delight, then, to find the septuagenarian poet in the 1990s musing

"Two loves at my age, isn't it absurd?" One of these loves (though their relationship was not sexual) was with twenty-four year old muse Mark Smith, and the few letters to Smith are the most joyous of the book. Love intensifies the qualities that shine throughout elsewhere: Morgan's candour, his generosity, his wit, his knowledge and, above all, his unbounded enthusiasm and excitability. In the final letter to Smith published here, the poet also reflects on his encroaching mortality:

"if a few poems survived it would be enough – I'd be in the poems – anything else would be defying the law of death. I also have the stubborn irrational belief (but is it wholly irrational) that everything we do is somehow written into the fabric of the universe and cannot be destroyed even if it cannot be accessed."

Thanks to the work of McGonigal and Coyle, now a little more of Morgan can be accessed, irrationality notwithstanding. It is an important volume, and a fascinating portrait of a restless and remarkable mind.

– *Neko Karenin*

Turn, Try to Breathe and Turn

Jellyfish
Janice Galloway

Freight Books, RRP£12.99 169 pp

"You can see through them ... into their guts."

On a seaside trip, a young boy is briefly distressed coming across rows of dead jellyfish stranded by the tide. His mother explains what the little round gummy patties are, then fights to conceal her consternation when he spots one that has met a crueler fate. The title story of Janice Galloway's brilliant new collection finds wise and watchful Monica helping her four-year-old learn what is safe to try and what is risky, so he can leave her, running off into his own life, though her heart is in her mouth.

Seeing into the 'guts' of sex, love and parenthood across all fourteen stories, Galloway contests David Lodge's assertion that "Literature is mostly about having sex and not much about having children; life's the other way round." And she has done so successfully: the collection was long-listed for the Frank O'Connor International Short Story Award.

Life, seen from the parental angle, is not any less risky. The children (and adult children) we meet are, or have been, in danger of varying kinds; injury, accident, benign neglect or, in the case of the story 'turned', much worse ensues. For example, 'almost 1948', published in Gutter 12, 'reimagines' a very ill Eric Blair working on *Nineteen Eighty Four* on Jura with his son and sister, following his wife's death. In 'distance', Martha watches helplessly as her son Peter, just three, runs into a sheet glass table, splitting open his head.

"A towel pressed to his forehead soaked as soon as it touched, blood forcing up through the fibres. As though the wound had been made by a cutlass. She cradled his face, hands running like a butcher's, as his eyes rolled and the screaming went on, and on, and on."

"It's alright," Martha croons ... "Let mummy take it." All the pain and tears, the fear and Martha's fight to "take it" throughout, leave the reader pondering, as Monica did in 'jellyfish', how we best protect our children, assess their hurt and offer comfort, while still gently turning them free to live their lives and take on risks. And, how to manage the same for ourselves? George Orwell, on Jura, carries his son Richard "bloody as a fox" to the doctor for stitches, but resents being advised to stop pushing himself so hard physically, to finish his book.

As Orwell is soon to be, many of the parents are lost, absent or dead. Dads or mums, including Martha, leave or have left already. Characters felled by emotional pain, still try every which way to keep on keeping on. Martha, on a trip to Jura, is confronted with a damaged and terrified wild creature, heaving in physical agony. Despite her frozen grief and the bloody gore in front of her, she manages to give (and therefore, strangely, receive) some comfort in the crisis. The trick, echoing Galloway's now classic debut novel title, is once again, just to keep breathing. Stay present. Here.

In 'turned', we witness a daughter who can't stay present, can't bear her own name and has horror echoing endlessly in her head. The story is a masterpiece in capturing incoherent trauma, transforming fragments on the page into a vivid searing portrayal of the tricks minds play when trying to making sense of the incomprehensible. Seeing an arm splayed on the ground, the girl urges herself frantically to run, "Turn. Try to breathe and turn. Turn."

And we can turn away, remembering with gratitude the more light-hearted, sensual stories, the laugh out loud moments, and applauding the magic of the last lines that surprise.

– *Jabberwocky*

Back in Nagasaki

A Dictionary of Mutual Understanding
Jackie Copleton

Hutchinson, RRP £12.99, 304pp

In 2011, in order to raise money to help the survivors of the Japanese triple disaster, Cargo Publishing brought out *A Thousand Cranes*, an anthology of Scottish writers, including several now making bigger waves. One of those is Jackie Copleton, whose debut novel A *Dictionary of Mutual Understanding*, delivers on the promise of that earlier short story.

Amaterasu Takahashi and her husband Kenzo fled to America in the aftermath of the Nagasaki atomic bombing. Elderly and widowed, she is resigned to a life with only a bottle and regrets for companionship. The arrival of a man who claims to be her dead grandson, Hideo, overturns the barricades she's built between herself and the past. Her daughter, Yuko, along with Hideo, died on August 9th 1945. Yuko's husband Shige never made it back from the war. This seems enough sadness and horror for one life, but further layers are about to be peeled back to reveal deeper hurts and further wrongs.

At the heart of this book lies the question all survivors of tragedy ask – why me? The answer Amaterasu is seeking in the bottle is simple – if I had done things differently, would my daughter still be alive today? The twisted roads that led Yuko to be in Urakami Cathedral, ground zero for the blast, at exactly that moment, are contained in the diaries she left behind and in the letters the man who claims to be Hideo carries from his adopted parents.

A Dictionary of Mutual Understanding is a love letter to Nagasaki. The city is something of an oddity in Japan – the open window left when the country closed its doors for hundreds of years – and Copleton's descriptions endow it with the otherworldly quality Kazuo Ishiguro brought to the city in his early work. Yet mixed in with the sentimentality is an unblinking exploration of Nagasaki's all too physical aspects. She takes us into the filthy underbelly of the 'floating world', where women are objects to be enjoyed then cast aside, and where promises last only as long as the sake.

The book takes its title from the snippets of *An English Dictionary of Japanese Culture* which start each chapter. It's a clever device that allows Copleton to clarify aspects of Japanese culture readers may be unfamiliar with, but they also act as threads for Amaterasu, breadcrumbs trailing back to a world destroyed by 'pikadon' – the onomatopoeic equivalent of 'flash-bang'.

The details are vivid and vital. There is so much heartbreak in this book, so much anger and regret, that Copleton lets events speak for themselves, allowing her prose to dwell on the sensual realities. From children torturing insects moments before the blast to the prostitutes flashing their red under-kimonos, the novel is alive with vibrant, well-observed moments.

The bombing was a terrible end for millions, but countless others had to live on in the rubble and rebuild. Why me? What if? The past can disconnect us from the future. *A Dictionary of Mutual Understanding* is about letting go of those questions and finding peace in the absence of answers.

– *Totoro*

Something Fishy Going On

The Visitors
Simon Sylvester
Quercus Books, RRP £8.99, 368pp

Simon Sylvester's first novel *The Visitors* is set on the fictional Scottish island of Bancree where seventeen year old Flora finds herself an outcast. Cut free by her university-bound boyfriend and ostracised by the in crowd at school, she is counting down the days until she too can escape when the titular visitors arrive.

The newcomers, John Dobie and his daughter, Ailsa, move into the sole cottage on Dog Rock, a smaller island off the coast of Bancree, a final pebble before the raging ocean. This symbolism suits them, particularly John, an intense, menacing man who shows no interest in joining the small community. Ailsa, however, seems to be just another awkward teenager, and the two solitary girls quickly find each other.

People on Bancree are disappearing. At first the locals seek comfort in the transient nature of seasonal work and other forms of economic migration to account for the absences. But once a body has washed ashore, the islanders must face reality: a murderer is in their midst. Local suspicion is directed at the incomers, but Flora is convinced of their innocence and determined to protect them.

The Visitors is ostensibly a plot driven thriller, a whodunit with enough twists, turns and cliff-hangers to keep the reader guessing, but it can also be enjoyed as a moving piece of literary fiction. The descriptions of the island and the febrile gossip-fuelled town bring to mind Iain Banks at his sociological best, while fans of Linda Cracknell's *Call of the Undertow* or Amy Sackville's *Orkney* may recognise certain recurring themes.

Simon Sylvester's first book was the Twitter fiction collection *140 Characters* (Cargo, 2011) and the sentence expertise he perfected there has transferred well to the novel form. The prose is tight and lean yet lyrical and expressive, the characters pinned by a single exquisitely chosen adjective. As always with his writing (for example the stories published in Gutter over a number of issues), the prose remains subservient to the story, elucidating and entertaining without ever straying into self-indulgence.

Storytelling itself is a trope – indeed one of the characters, Izzy, is a shanachie, a storyteller – and Scottish folklore is carefully woven into the fabric of the novel. Everyone in Bancree has their own yarn, but stories are never just stories. These tales inadvertently reveal shattering truths. As in all the best mystery novels, the characters give themselves away through their choice of falsehood. Every lie has honesty at its heart.

The Visitors is a novel about alienation and loneliness. The imagery is of outliers – the island off the coast of another island, the storyteller living in a hut made from flotsam, the bullied girl with deep inner strength who knows that deliverance is merely a matter of months away. Characters and relationships are defined by distance.

Of these loners, The Dobies are the most alienated. As suspicion grows even the reader is tempted to turn against them. Yet it's the outsiders who provide clarity and objectivity. The storyteller Izzy knows more about Bancree's history than the locals. Ailsa introduces Flora to wonders on her doorstep she never knew existed. The solitary have time to watch and learn, but observation changes both observed and observer.

The characters we pity are the ones who cannot cope with loneliness, with rejection; who project strength as a defence. Flora learns that the moments we share with others can be spectacular, but it's self-confidence that gives us strength. Each of us are islands, entire of ourselves.

– *Totoro*

News From Somewhere

The Limits of the World
Andrew Raymond Drennan

Cargo Publishing, RRP £8.99, 266pp

It's late 2011 in the Democratic People's Republic of Korea. Han is a recently promoted officer of North Korea's Ministry of Communications about to begin another assignment as a tour guide for the country's Western visitors. These stage-managed encounters with foreigners only deepen his acute sense of loneliness and encourage one very dangerous vice. Among his meagre possessions are items so threatening to the state they could earn him imprisonment and execution: Han reads Western books.

The tourists arriving from the outside world bring their own secrets too. Ben and Hal are undercover documentary-makers who think a scoop in North Korea will be easier than another war zone. Han's occasional moments of candour lead them to suspect he's their best chance of capturing the true face of the Hermit Kingdom, if, that is, they are willing to risk his life.

Andrew Raymond Drennan's ambitious third novel is a welcome variation on the ever popular theme of dystopia. If readers ever tire of imagining nightmare societies in which the poor starve while feigning devotion to an absolute leader, they need only remember that twenty-five million people still call North Korea home. While books about this rogue state tend to feed the factual appetite, in common with

Adam Johnson's Pulitzer Prize-winning *The Orphan Master's Son*, Drennan shows that a deeply researched work of imagination can do more than report back.

Han is the perfect companion on our journey into this closed world precisely because he is one of us, a reader. Through him we see familiar books living precarious new lives: Austen, Conrad, Dickens and Kafka hide under a floorboard in his apartment like refugees, or explosives. On encountering *Nineteen Eighty-Four*, Han identifies with Winston Smith in ways we never could. He reads for pleasure and to know he is not alone, but when he finds himself radicalised in the company of a fellow reader, she is someone he surely cannot trust.

The novel's unconventional chapter headings and occasionally mixed perspectives are the only hurdles to the story as it accelerates to thriller pace in its final act. At the heart of this lean and energetic novel is a rather beautiful meditation on loss. In a country where public grief is held in reserve for the passing of the Dear Leader, private grieving (like reading) is an act of resistance. Han has lost his parents and sister, yet is not authorised to mourn them. The journalists also carry complicated bereavements with them. Hal, a practicing Christian, fixates on footage he shot in Sudan of a mob killing a man he couldn't save, while Ben is yet to process the loss of the beloved father who inspired him. These griefs forge a common humanity between them.

The title of the book alludes to Ludwig Wittgenstein: "The limits of my language mean the limits of my world." While physical boundaries can only be established or exceeded by force, works of language (like this one) reveal a world without borders, a true People's Republic. In other words: books do not set us free, they remind us that we already are.

– Marlinspike

"All Kinds of Corset-Related Deaths"

The Hourglass Factory
Lucy Ribchester

Simon & Schuster, RRP £7.99, 504 pp

Lucy Ribchester's debut novel *The Hourglass Factory* is an action-packed murder-mystery that romps through 1912 Edwardian London: from Tarot to tight-lacing, suffragettes to circus acts. Onto the scene steps Frankie, an intrepid independent woman in tweed trousers, determined to make her living as a journalist. When she is sent to interview a trapeze artist, she discovers a much bigger story and adventure ensues.

A surprising medley of tones emerges as Ribchester engages with this fascinating historical milieu. The Suffragettes are treated with the rigour and seriousness that they deserve – both window-smashing and force-feeding are brought back to life in unflinching detail. Other scenes offer surprisingly moving moments, such as that of suffragettes being sentenced while their supporters heckle the judge with cries of "shame". By way of contrast, the sub-plot concerning Inspector Primrose of the suffragette squad presents a more nuanced perspective as he wrestles the inner conflict of his duty to uphold the law and pressure from his hideously sexist colleagues and superiors. His instinct for justice makes him baulk at the way he sees women being treated and his character explores a rarely-voiced ambivalence in historical fiction of this era.

Such realistic re-enactments of the suffragette debate are counterbalanced by the book's more delightfully macabre elements. In one memorable scene Frankie visits a morgue with jars of pickled body parts on display. Quizzing the mortician for leads Frankie is told that, "You get all kinds of corset-related deaths". This generous helping of gruesome detail adds darker undertones to a rollicking plot in which Frankie and friends have to piece together clues, escape sticky situations, and foil villains. The narrative also has its fair share of tongue-in-cheek moments, such as the hilariously suggestive pink and toothless snake that performs with exotic-dancer Milly.

Milly, who has left a life of upper-class privilege to make her living as an exotic dancer, is typical of the clearly-drawn, larger-than-life characters of *The Hourglass*. There's also Twinkle, a melodramatic retired courtesan, and the enigmatic Ebony Diamond, trapeze artist and suffragette. Further back-stories are hinted at and would be welcomed, especially Frankie's past. The mysteries of the plot unfold, clue by clue, but Frankie remains opaque, apart from a few teasing references to her childhood. What drove her to become a cross-dressing lady journalist? I wanted to find that out just as much as I wanted to find out who dunnit.

The only other minor distraction is the few sticky bits of dialogue and description. Sometimes it's not clear who's saying what or why they're saying it, and some of the more crowded scenes are described in a disjointed way that doesn't convey a cohesive impression. However, overall, the story was strong enough to carry me through these minor distractions and made for an enjoyable read, especially the playful Calvin Harris reference, if you spot it.

– Héloïse

Shoot the Canon?

Double Bill
Andy Jackson – Editor

Red Squirrel Publishing, RRP £10.00, 192pp

Double Bill is the sequel to 2012's successful poetry anthology, *Split Screen,* incorporating themes such as; film, television, sport, art, dance, and even adverts. The editor, Andy Jackson, has a stellar line-up which includes; W.N. Herbert, Helen Mort, George Szirtes, Jo Bell, Tony Curtis, and Helen Ivory. The anthology's structure is akin to an old-fashioned visit to the cinema; three distinct parts interspersed with short poems about adverts. Jackson presents poems in pairs; the links are sometimes amusing, for example 'Crossroads Motel' and the 'Bates Motel' from *Psycho*. This strict pairing results in blank pages which can be jarring. However,

Jackson is to be congratulated on achieving a gender balance, and poets from Northern Britain are well-represented, as are those published by Red Squirrel.

Many poetry collections rely on a foreknowledge of the literary canon or assume a classical arts education. Consequently, too many potential readers pick up that important first book of poetry and put it down again sharpish, bamboozled by the contents. I defy anyone to pick up *Double Bill* without finding something to charm or disarm. The literary canon is not to be abandoned, but vibrant alternatives are necessary as a way in for new readers and for the occasional book to read by the pool. I haven't had so many laugh-out-loud moments from a poetry book since Henry Normal's *Nude Modelling For The Afterlife*: and that wasn't yesterday, or even this millennium. Special plaudits go to Kevin Cadwallender for his take on Eric and Ernie and Sheila Templeton for revealing her surreal passion for *Thing* in 'The Addams Family', "I *wanted* him, the way he beckoned, the way / he crooked that long forefinger…"

Comedy is counterbalanced by poignancy. 'Benny's Crossroad Blues' by Martin Figura starts with an amusing look at *Crossroads* and leaves us at Nick Drake's gravestone. 'The Black Tapestry of Amy Winehouse' by Janette Ayachi is beautifully woven. There is also critical commentary on popular culture; Joan Hewitt provides an affectionately scathing account of *Woman's Hour*; Tim Turnbull sends up *Strictly Come Dancing* and McGuire takes on *Judge Judy*.

Some subjects may be unfamiliar to readers, however, fortunately Jackson has included subject headings so you have something to Google if you've never heard of Pearl Jam, Les Kellett, Prince Buster, the Hacienda or Madchester 'The Ghost Train – a Twinned Sonnet' by John Glenday brilliantly describes the complex bond between the Boulting Brothers; "When you looked into my face, you looked into a mirror, / and smiled, and took my shoulder, held me safe, then pushed me over." This poem works even if you don't know these identical twins from the films. However, this is not true of all the poems. Irene Hossack's excellent poem, *Fairy Liquid*, does lose some of its emotional charge if you haven't watched those excruciating 60's adverts with their remorseless exploitation of an idealised mother-daughter relationship.

In his introduction, Jackson flirts with the possibility of a third volume. We need an anthology of popular Scottish culture. There is so much scope: The One O'Clock Gang; The White Heather Club; Take the High Road; Taggart; The Steamie; Chewin the Fat; Still Game; Scotch & Wry. It would be amusing and culturally defining to read poems about Rab C. Nesbitt, Elaine C. Smith, the Proclaimers, Lulu, Sean Connery, Billy Connolly and Karen Dunbar. And how about Tunnocks Tea Cakes and Irn Bru in the interval? Come on Andy Jackson!

– *Kanga Kangeroo*

Lifting the Dank Curtain

Killochries
Jim Carruth

Freight Books, RRP £8.99, 160pp

I really shouldn't like this book. Sheep play a significant role, there are whole pages devoted to quotes from St John's gospel and one of the two main characters is staunchly religious. It's a 'verse novella'. It sounds awful, doesn't it? Yet it is wonderful.

The protagonist, an angry urbanite, has a legacy of drink and money trouble and 'something not true' about him. He goes to spend time drying out, escaping perhaps, on a remote hill farm with an older relative. This relative is a pious shepherd, and the protagonist dries out with the shepherd, his bedridden mother, three dogs, some cows, chickens and sheep. The story happens over the course of a year and, season by season, the relationship between the two men unfolds. There is mutual scorn and inevitable conflict, and then spring comes. The troubled poet gains respect, first for the shepherd, and then, for himself.

The narrative is simple, gently paced and told through a series of short-lined poems in sparse, clear language. It feels utterly assured, like the telling of a parable. From the first few brushstrokes, we know we are in the hands of a masterful painter of nature and rural people. Here, for a flavour of the clarity of writing and vivid characterisation, is the poet's first meeting with the shepherd;

"He looks me over –
a new ram
he might bid for
at some local market....

He tuts and turns,
expects me
to come to heel."

Here's an attempt at fence maintenance:

"Tight wire snaps,
lashes back,

its ravel and grasp
wraps fast."

Such taut, crisp language paints a picture of a stark place and an austere life. Reminiscent of some of MacCaig's desolation at what he perceived as the end of crofting, this story honours the shepherd's doomed livelihood. Although he doesn't get into the politics of this demise (which is perhaps a shame), the poet asks:

"But what use am I to him?
My poems cannot stretch a helping hand,
my words will never fill his run-down barn,
my lines cannot defend his fragile land."

Such despair about the demise of hill farming, and the resultant grief, loss and suffering are leavened by humour. For example, there is a superb vignette of a country fair. At another point, the city poet's first attempt to milk the cow is so bad that the shepherd remarks, 'A'll mebbe hae ma tea black the night.' The shepherd speaks in a 'dank curtain' of Scots, his words few but always significant and, although not always necessary, there is an excellent glossary.

Religious disagreement between the two characters drives the story, yet this is not a critique of dogma. It explores with real open-heartedness what faith might be able to offer: even to a hardened non-believer. Wild nature is a balance to the religion of the shepherd, and an alternative source of solace and inspiration. At one point a waterfall skeins across the page, like a kind of prayer to the wild for freedom of mind and expression. There is an echo of Ted Hughes in the fox that appears repeatedly as a symbol of poetry and a spirit presence throughout.

This is not only a story, but a sequence of delicately crafted poems. The characters grow and change which is an exceptional feat across a volume of poetry. It even won over this sheep-loathing atheist.

– *Spectacled Bear*

The Pleasure of Pleasure

Know yr Stuff: Poems on Hedonism
Calum Rodger

Tapsalteerie, RRP £5.00, 32pp

The thirty-two page pamphlet is a wonderfully flexible athlete without which the world of small press publishing would be seriously diminished. It is ideally suited for polemic, personal artistic statement, poetic experiment and many other handy do-it-yourself items. Calum Rodger uses the space and format extremely well, making a valuable contribution to the pamphleteering tradition.

'Know Yr Stuff' takes the reader gleefully into hedonism with breezy zest and knowing wry humour. Given that life is a mix of highs and lows, what we're given by Rodger is mostly the up-beat side in his sequence of eight poems. Witness the opening lines from the eponymous 'know yr stuff',

> "When I was a boy
> they gave us at school
> a little blue book
> it was well fucking cool"

The poem floats along on its decasyllabic rhythm in what are essentially rhyming couplets. Appropriately for a piece set in the class-room, the rhythmic ease is suggestive of nursery rhyme. This opening poem sets a narrative tone and trajectory for what follows. However, we don't meet with the structured rhyme scheme of childhood again, "for that was the day / Metaphysics arrived", propelling us forward into something resembling adulthood, where one may find oneself in a "pesky existential void", drowning in "pleasure", "drunk" – or some combination of these.

For those who like long titles Rodger serves up 'the worst of my faults is a certain impatient gaiety of disposition', and for those who like one word titles there is 'pleasure'. This reader found 'pleasure' the most bold and formally interesting poem in the collection. It is part syllogistic-list-poem, part concrete poem and part prose,

suggesting unlikely connections with humour and philosophical depth. Epicurus wrote, 'we recognize pleasure as the first good innate in us, and from pleasure we begin every act of choice and avoidance, and to pleasure we return again', and Rodger hints at this notion with his recurrent motif of "*cue-routine-reward*" which occurs in the second and penultimate poems.

In 'know yr stuff' and 'last poem' the theme of a highly significant association with another human being arises, so the collection has both balance and artistic intelligence. Rodger depicts a masculinity which is happily absent of violence and other well-known ostensibly 'male' stupidities. There is a grasping towards universal pleasure and a lyrical smile in the colourfully titled 'sexual positions with imaginary girlfriends':

> "*Spring for lust*
> bud in a blanket
> *summer for passion*
> bloom in shadow
> autumn for fucking
> all four seasons
> *winter for love*
> one dark morning"

and in 'because I am drunk', the following lines on trust are presented four times in step fashion across the page:

> "trust
> trust the set to adjust itself
> itself"

Are they a sigh of acceptance, an expression of hope, a plea for 'trust' in life's pleasures? Rodger opens poetic possibilities with ease

that makes writing good poetry look like a breeze. It is a pleasure to be in his company.
– *Towser*

Alight Here As Often As Possible

Do Not Alight Here Again
Rachel McCrum
Stewed Rhubarb, RRP £5.00, 20pp

Ire & Salt
Jenny Lindsay
Stewed Rhubarb, RRP £5.00, 24pp

Rachel McCrum and Jenny Lindsay are perhaps best-known for Rally and Broad, their innovative and highly acclaimed cabaret of spoken word and music which has been delighting audiences in Edinburgh since 2012, and Glasgow since last year. Their contribution to Scotland's burgeoning spoken word scene cannot be understated; nor, indeed, can their great skill as performers of their own work. However, the flourishing of the performance poetry scene has given rise to a common question among Scottish poets; are you a stage poet or a page poet? Happily, McCrum and Lindsay prove this to be a false dichotomy with *Do Not Alight Here Again* and *Ire & Salt*. In both performance and print, their work glows with a lyrical intimacy and refreshing directness, borne out in two of the most immediate and compelling poetic voices in Scotland today. Demonstrating their fidelity to the idea that stage/page is no either/or, the poets launched their pamphlets with performances at either side of the central belt. At *The Old Hairdresser's* in Glasgow, the evening's 'stage' – a solitary microphone against a bare brick backdrop – could not be more appropriate. McCrum's first poem, 'Please Do Not Listen to the Sound of My Voice', opens:

"Hello.
I am here to perform for you.
I do not have an instrument that you can see
but I have practised.
I am here
To read some poems I have written."

No need for a *visible* 'instrument'. Rather, this unadorned but carefully measured opening points to the crucial quality of *presence*; 'I am here'. Both poets playfully tease at the limits of this idea: between print and performance, reality and fiction, history and everyday living, memory and hope.

McCrum's Northern Irish background binds the question of presence to memory, both personal, as with the "message / signed off 'your proud da'", and cultural, as the poet laments how her "fathers [...] have told our story badly!" In either case, these reflections have a tactile quality: 'salt, bitter and vital' and 'sand' that 'breathed'. On stage and on page, these words have *body*.

Lindsay's approach is more defiant – belligerent even – taking to the stage as if staging a coup. Her presence is rooted firmly in the historical present, struggling with vital questions of national and cultural identity in these economically, institutionally and existentially volatile times. See, for example, the acute diagnosis of millennial malaise in 'b. 1979+':

> "question marks stop
> home is where you
> can build what you want
> and we will, b. 1979+
> pass the wine"

Elsewhere, the political polemics of 'A 'Very Scottish' Spoken Word Provocation' juxtapose violently –perfectly – with the staccato confessionalism of 'Today'. In print, the latter's prose lines stutter and cascade through contorted repetitions and internal rhymes ("Today is a 4. Smudge-drunk, swampy-mush-fug 4. Fuck the shops. Today is a 4."). At *The Old Hairdresser's*, Lindsay's frank and heartrending delivery make it the most powerful moment of the evening. Her coup is real: for a politically-rooted self-expression that many would doubtless prefer mute.

Both McCrum and Lindsay are adept at building an intimacy – and tension – with an audience, so it is reassuring that neither intimacy nor tension is lost on the printed page. Performance and pamphlet are complement and counterpoint, and these collections important poetic documents of our time from two of Scotland's finest cultural innovators. Go and see them perform; and be sure to pick up both pamphlets from the book stall on your way home.

– *Neko Karenin*

Spitting Spleen into the Streets

Scottish Spleen
Edited by Tom Hubbard, James W. Underhill and Stewart Sanderson

Tapsalteerie (£5.00, 34 pages)

Scottish Spleen is a scots-language translation of a selection of Baudelaire's prose poems, collected posthumously as 'le Spleen de Paris,' with a couple of better-known works from Les Fleurs du Mal also included. The small collection comes with a comparatively lengthy foreword making a passionate case for the validity of the work of putting Baudelaire into scots, arguing that to do so brings across the demotic and the vital in the Frenchman''s work. The poems demand you approach them wholeheartedly, that you accept the artifice of 19th century French rendered in to 21st century Scots. James W. Underhill's "Crood-bathin" is about the ability of a poet, in a crowd, to be "able at will to be baith hissel or any onybody else." This is what the best of the poets do here, embodying a long-dead cosmopolitan French Poet in their own work, a process which, in his own introduction, Underhill likens to the Scottish hallowe'en tradition of guising. He also claims that the syntax of modern Scots has more in common with Baudelaire's original French than some standard English does. This may or may not be true, but certainly the best of them do fizz and sparkle with life, feeling more conversational and less hidebound than the equivalent English renderings may. They are scabrous and foul in places, tender and surprising. Tom Hubbard's 'The Dug and The Scent-Bottle' is a highlight, which demands to be read aloud to anyone in earshot with a rhythm that the best poems in this volume share: urgent, conversational and beautifully suited to the scots vocabulary. The translations are from a number of pens in different flavours of scots, with spelling and orthography not standardised, allowing each poet's voice, or rather, each poet's version of the voice of Baudelaire, to come through. Despite this, the collection feels unified in purpose and tone.

It is a real shame that Robert R Calder's translation of 'Chacun sa Chimère' as 'Ilkane his ain Chimaera' should render *"la surface arrondie de la planète se dérobe à la curiosité du regard humain,"* as 'The planet taks aff her veils for the human ee's inquisitiveness,' which seems to be a mangling of the verb *se dérober* (to slip away, occlude) with its opposite ('taks aff her veils,' here) It doesn't make much sense in context and mars what is otherwise a surprisingly faithful collection. There are many turns of phrase I suspected to be cut from translators' whole cloth which turn out to have a fitting analogue in the original, which is pleasing. All of this is for nothing though, if the poetry does not connect, through these layers of accretion: of being a translation, of being a translation into scots. Thankfully the poetry does connect, on the whole. Tom Hubbard's 'Invitatioun to the Stravaig' has a sincerity and a tenderness to it that makes it feel spontaneous, and punches through the patina of age and reputation to deliver a gruff emotional impact.

An odd collection then that requires a willingness from readers – similar to that of Tapsalteerie in putting it out in the first place – a willingness to revivify the hidebound Baudelaire of leatherbound anthologies and send him spitting spleen into the streets. On these terms, it succeeds.

– *Sredni Vashtar*

Journey as Poem

The Road North
Alec Finlay and Ken Cockburn

Shearsman, £9.95, 136pp

In 1689 the poets Matsuo Bashō and Kawai Sora embarked on a journey to the Oku region of Japan, in the North. Their trip formed the basis of *Oku no Hosomichi*, Bashō's haibun prose/ haiku hybrid, blending travel observation, philosophical speculation, personal reflection and moments of sublime poetic distillation. Bashō's text forms the inspiration and textual hinterland for *the road north*, Alec Finlay and Ken Cockburn's new collection of poems inspired by a journey around Scotland, including Perthshire, Argyll, Lochaber, Lochalsh, and the Outer Hebrides.

Finlay and Cockburn's project reflects one of Bashō's intentions in undertaking the original journey, which was to visit places that feature in the writings of older Japanese poets, connecting these touchstones of past literature to his own technically exquisite and revolutionary approach to haikai. In their twenty-first century Scottish version, Finlay and Cockburn reimagine this vital link with poetic forebears by using *Oku no Hosomichi* as a guidebook or map to psychogeographically explore their own deep norths. The book begins, as Bashōs does, with a question; perhaps the most fitting introduction to a poetic sequence that is so much about exploration and inquiry rather than answers and definitions.

The range of poetic forms explored across *the road north* as it riffs in and out of *Oku no Hosomichi* is breath-taking and even exhilarating, as though the language of the poets is responding to the diverse undulations of the landscape itself. There are delicious haiku: "if the sea knew what / it was it wouldn't / keep coming back", counterpoised by extended poetic explorations, in which, for example, the poets find "time for a skinny dip" on "wee gravel beaches / each just big enough for one", "inviting an act, a rite / done right". There's a circular visual poem, some list poems and incantatory chants. In some, the conversation and collaboration of the poets spills joyfully over into the poems: "you climbed / and you climbed, Ken! / Ach how you climbed!"

One of the characteristics of Bashō's poetics is the freshness of his observation, as his emotional reactions to the world observed take many surprising turns. This is a characteristic which many of the poems in the road north also share, perhaps for me most pronouncedly in 'an evening walk, Longmaddy, South Uist', where the moon on water is observed with such clarity that suddenly an image of it seems truly surprising:

"constant in phases
the incremental moon
gets a good washing
in the waves".

Solitary examples of superlative lyric expression don't give a sense, though, of the effect of reading *the road north* as a book, as a journey and as a pointer toward a wider journey through text and through life. The great American poet Cid Corman, who lived in Japan and translated the *Oku no Hosomichi* once wrote of Bashō that his poetry "evokes a context and wants one. These are not instances of lyricism but cries of their occasion, of some one intently passing through a world". While the particular cultural context of contemporary Scotland is important to the book, by tying their poetic pilgrimage across continents and centuries to Bashō's similar journey, Finlay and Cockburn remind us that the moon washing itself in the waves is the same moon that Bashō depicts (in Corman's translation) as "dripping / in storm-fraught waves". The same moon, maybe, but seen and experienced differently. Lyrical, expansive and inspiring, *the road north* is an important book, not least for reintroducing and reimagining Bashō's poetics into a Scottish context.

– *Speedwell*

Dear Gutter

I've very close to my mother but we can't stop fighting.

I'm a 38 year old woman and my marriage came to an end a couple of years ago. My mother has been very supportive throughout the whole mess but now the dust has settled we can't stop fighting with each other. I've always been very close to my Mum, particularly after her own relationship with my Dad ended in my teens. We're best friends, and spend a lot of time in each other's company. In my twenties I married a man who initially seemed loving but was subsequently unfaithful, something too hurtful for me to recover from. After I found him out there was a lot of anguish. We tried to make it work but things were never the same again, I'd lost all trust in him, and eventually I asked him to leave. Throughout our problems my Mum provided good advice and was hugely helpful in looking after our son. But now I'm on my own, and slowly emerging from the trauma of the breakup, we constantly bicker. She seems to find fault with everything I do, is petty, anxious and wants to make decisions for me and my son. I think she blames me for the failure of my marriage. How do I get things back to the way they were?

Gutter says:

Without being trite, it's unlikely that things will ever be the same again. However, this will probably be a good thing.

Firstly, it's very unlikely that your mother blames you for the end of your marriage. Parents are naturally protective of their offspring and wish the best for them. The breakdown may have awakened long-buried feelings related to her relationship with your father that are making her fearful. However, she may also feel a degree of responsibility for the breakdown, seeing it as history repeating itself, the result of her own past failures. Your mother may not have acknowledged this to herself yet so, if you choose to broach the subject, tread carefully.

But, perhaps, as you get yourself back on your feet emotionally, the dynamic between you and your mother is changing, and this shift is creating conflict. While it seems like she is picking on you, she may not be so very different to how she's always been. Maybe it's you that's changed and she's finding it difficult to adjust?

One of the most important things about families is leaving them. I'm not talking about your ex, or your father, but about you and your relationship with your mother. Sometimes a close relationship with a parent maintains the child-adult axis established in childhood and stops the relationship developing into an adult-to-adult exchange. This is most obvious in a physical lack of separation, where the child remains in the family home well into adulthood, continuing their role as a dependent both financially and emotionally. However, it can just as easily be the result of an unconsciously controlling, dependent parent, regardless of where the child ends up living.

Some parents exert control through conditional love – 'be good for me', 'do well for me', 'always be there for me'. The implication (and tragically sometimes the reality) is that if the child fails to measure up then love will be withdrawn. This fosters anxiety and low self-esteem in the child. They are not worthy of unconditional love. It appears that love and self-worth can only be achieved through pleasing others. Other parents exert control through helplessness – addictive, self-destructive behaviours, emotional incontinence – forcing their child to become the adult in the relationship, providing physical or emotional support beyond their years, but stunting long-term emotional growth.

I'd ask you to consider how you relate to your mother and how she relates to you. Who calls the shots? Who does what they're told? How has the relationship developed over the years since your father left or has it remained the same? I wonder if, following your own separation, you're now discovering a new-found sense of independence and that's rocking the boat.

It might be worth taking the time to unpack what happened between you and your ex. In an ideal world you would be able to do this together, but it's rare for a couple who separated acrimoniously to put aside their differences and undertake such a process. However, with the drama of saving the relationship out of the way, it can be very rewarding. It can allow you both to gain a deeper understanding of what went wrong, enabling you to forgive each other and, more importantly, yourselves. Otherwise, spend time, preferably with professional help, looking closely at the relationship in detail, so you understand the choices you made from the very start and why you made them. It may be that some of the things that happened mirrored the ups and downs of your parents' marriage. It'd also be worth thinking about where your real emotional allegiances lay, with your partner or your best friend, your Mum?

A close, supportive relationship with one or both parents is commendable, so long as it's not at the expense our own decision-making. Ultimately, it's essential for all of us to be given the space and freedom away from our parents to become fully functioning, responsible adults. As a mother, this is something I'm sure you'll want for your own child when he approaches adulthood.

Contributor Biographies

Donald Adamson poet and translator from Finnish. Co-founder *Markings*; winner Herald Millennium Competition; collections: *From Coiled Roots* (Indigo Dreams), *Glamourie* (Indigo Dreams, forthcoming).

Claire Askew's prizewinning debut collection *This changes things* is forthcoming from Bloodaxe in 2016. She blogs at: onenightstanzas.com

Fran Baillie takes delight in searching for new Scots words and has had work published in *Gutter, Prole, GladRag, Lunar* and many others.

Sinothile Baloyi Zimbabwean born, she initially made Edinburgh her Scottish home before being lured west to Glasgow. This is her first published work.

Stephanie Brown has an MLitt in Creative Writing from Glasgow University and works as a subtitler.

Andrew Blair is a comedian and poet. He says 'deconstruction' but means 'wide bastard'. Blair is the Godfather of Edinburgh Poetry.

Peter Burnett is the author of *Scotland or No, #freetopiary, The Supper Book, Odium, The Studio Game* and other titles.

Ron Butlin is a former Edinburgh Makar. His new collection, *The Magicians of Scotland*, will be published in July.

Jim Carruth is the current Poet Laureate of Glasgow. His first full collection *Killochries* was published by Freight in April 2015.

Ben Critchley is a bookseller, poet, translator and layabout, hurtling towards thirty with little to show for it.

R.A. Davis was born in Edinburgh in 1983. He grew up in Kent and North Wales and belongs to Glasgow.

Christine De Luca writes (mainly) poetry in English and Shetlandic, now translated into many languages. She is the current Edinburgh Makar.

Leonie M. Dunlop is a writer and toponymist who is often found looking for lost place-names in Berwickshire.

Sally Evans' most recent book is *The Grecian Urn*, in the University of Bucharest's series *Bibliotecha Universalis*. She is a previous contributor to *Gutter*.

Rodge Glass is author of six books, and winner of a Somerset Maugham award. His next novel is *Once a Great Leader*.

Pippa Goldschmidt's latest book is a short story collection, *The Need for Better Regulation of Outer Space*.

Mandy Haggith is a writer and environmental activist. Her most recent novel is Bear Witness.

Allan Harkness Look out... a) everything is warring competition again, b) for each other, c) night is falling. Answers in poems please: few, brief, lifelong.

Jason Henderson Heavily influenced by political and societal issues, Lanarkshire's Jason Henderson is a writer of both English and the Scots leid.

Kate Hendry lives and writes in Edinburgh. Her first collection of poems will be published by Happenstance Press next year.

Colin Herd is a poet and Creative Writing lecturer. Publications include *too ok* (2011), *Glovebox* (2014) and *Oberwildling* (2015).

Andy Jackson writer and editor of poetry, has a new collection *A Beginner's Guide To Cheating* due on Red Squirrel Press in late 2015.

Vicki Jarrett is a novelist and short story writer from Edinburgh. Her collection, *The Way Out*, is published by Freight.

Doug Johnstone is an author, journalist and musician. He's written seven novels, umpteen short stories, five albums and two EPs.

Russell Jones is an Edinburgh-based writer and editor. His first full-length poetry collection is out with Freight Books in September 2015.

Henry King studied and taught English Literature at the University of Glasgow. He blogs at Between Sound And Sense (henrymking.blogspot.co.uk).

Joan Lennon a Canadian Scot, lives and writes in the Kingdom of Fife, in a flat overlooking the silvery Tay.

Liz Lochhead is an award-winning poet and playwright. She was appointed as the National Poet for Scotland in 2011.

Lindsay Macgregor co-hosts Platform poetry nights in the Stationmaster's bedroom at Ladybank and has a New Writer's Award 2015.

Neil Mackay is a multi-award winning investigative journalist, newspaper executive, non-fiction author, radio broadcaster and film-maker.

Rob A Mackenzie's latest collection is *The Good News* (Salt 2013). His next will contain seven poems about guinea pigs

Iain Maloney is from Aberdeen and lives in Japan. His novels *First Time Solo* and *Silma Hill* are available now

Ross McGregor is a previous recipient of the Scottish Book Trust New Writer's Award. He has had poetry published in *Gutter, New Writing Scotland* and *Algebra*.

Joe McInnes has had short stories published in *Gutter* and *New Writing Scotland*. He is currently working on his first novel.

Nick-e Melville *Lyrical Commands* is taken from nick-e melville's *The Imperative Commands*, his epic 365 page PhD thesis in progress.

Fiona Montgomery a graduate of Glasgow University's Creative Writing MLitt, is a freelance journalist and is writing a memoir.

Ian Newman graduated from Glasgow University in 2000 where he studied literature. He currently lives with his family in Kirriemuir.

Wendy Orr is winner of Mother's Milk Books Poetry Competition and has poems forthcoming in *Ink, Sweat and Tears* and *Lighthouse.*

Stuart A Paterson born 1966, lives by the Solway Coast, walks alot. *Border Lines* will be released by Indigo Dreams Publishing in August.

Stav Poleg's graphic-novel piece *Dear Penelope* (with artist Laura Gressani) was acquired by the Scottish National Gallery of Modern Art.

AP Pullan is originally from Yorkshire now residing in Ayrshire. Published in various magazines and anthologies. Currently working on a novel for children.

Eveline Pye has an international reputation for statistical poetry. Her collection *Smoke That Thunders* was published in May 2015 by Mariscat.

Calum Rodger is a Glasgow-based poet and scholar. His pamphlet *Know Yr Stuff: Poems on Hedonism* is published by Tapsalteerie.

Sue Reid Sexton's two novels are *Mavis's Shoe* and *Rue End Street*. She writes and escapes in a tiny campervan.

John Saunders is an Irish poet who has published two collections with Lapwing Press and New Binary Press. Google him now.

Stewart Sanderson is finishing a PhD at Glasgow. His first pamphlet, *Fios*, is published by Tapsalteerie Press: **www.tapsalteerie.co.uk**

Tim Turnbull lives near Dunkeld. He has a collection of short stories due from Red Squirrel Press in 2016.

Hamish Scott born in Edinburgh in 1960, now lives in Tranent where he writes poetry and prose in Scots.

Lynnda Wardle grew up in Johannesburg. Her work has appeared in *Gutter, thi wurd, NWS* and *Glasgow Review of Books* **www.lynndawardle.com**

George T Watt is Membership Secretar o the Scots Language Society an is a honrary memer o the Associacio dos Escritos do Amazonas in Brazil.